CATEGORICALLY INCORRECT

Also by A. Alan Borovoy

When Freedoms Collide:
The Case for Our Civil Liberties (1988)
Uncivil Obedience:
The Tactics and Tales of a Democratic Agitator (1991)
The New Anti-Liberals (1999)

CATEGORICALLY INCORRECT

Ethical Fallacies in Canada's War on Terror

A. Alan Borovoy

THE DUNDURN GROUP
TORONTO

Editor: Michael Carroll
Design: Alison Carr
Printer: University of Toronto Press

Library and Archives Canada Cataloguing in Publication

Borovoy, A. Alan
Categorically incorrect : ethical fallacies in Canada's war on terrorism / A. Alan Borovoy.

Includes bibliographical references and index.
ISBN 10: 1-55002-628-3
ISBN 13: 978-1-55002-628-3

1. Afghan War, 2001- --Canada.   2. Afghan War, 2001- --Moral and ethical aspects.
3. Democracy--Canada.   4. War on Terrorism, 2001- --Moral and ethical aspects.
5. Civil rights--Canada.   6. Canada--Foreign relations--1945-.   I. Title.

HV6433.C3B67 2006   303.6'250971   C2006-905968-3

1   2   3   4   5   10   09   08   07   06

Conseil des Arts   Canada Council   Canada   ONTARIO ARTS COUNCIL
du Canada   for the Arts   CONSEIL DES ARTS DE L'ONTARIO

We acknowledge the support of the Canada Council for the Arts and the Ontario Arts Council for our publishing program. We also acknowledge the financial support of the Government of Canada through the Book Publishing Industry Development Program and The Association for the Export of Canadian Books, and the Government of Ontario through the Ontario Book Publishers Tax Credit program, and the Ontario Media Development Corporation.

Care has been taken to trace the ownership of copyright material used in this book. The author and the publisher welcome any information enabling them to rectify any references or credits in subsequent editions.

J. Kirk Howard, President

Printed and bound in Canada.
Printed on recycled paper.
www.dundurn.com

Dundurn Press   Gazelle Book Services Limited   Dundurn Press
3 Church Street, Suite 500   White Cross Mills   2250 Military Road
Toronto, Ontario, Canada   High Town, Lancaster, England   Tonawanda, NY
M5E 1M2   LA1 4XS   U.S.A. 14150

CONTENTS

Acknowledgements

The impulse to write this book is attributable to a disquiet that engulfed me as Canada debated its response to the events of September 11, 2001 (9/11). I could not disgorge the sense that the debate was mired in critical fallacies. By chance, I happened to mention my discomfort to Patrick Luciani, an official of the Donner Canadian Foundation with whom I had lunch back in August 2002.

He reacted with the unexpected suggestion that I ask my organization, the Canadian Civil Liberties Association (CCLA), to prepare a grant proposal to his foundation for a book on the subject. The idea appealed to me, but it also created problems.

I wanted to write about international as well as domestic issues, but CCLA generally confines its activity to domestic matters. Thus, the organization declines to register on questions involving foreign policy. Indeed, there is no doubt that the leaders and members of CCLA entertain a wide variety of opinions on international issues. By contrast, the organization was quite active on the domestic front. It had been playing a vigorous role in addressing government initiatives to increase the legal weapons against terror. For these purposes, I had already spoken out many times as the organization's official representative.

But my impulse to write grew out of a strange asymmetry that I believed was influencing both the international and domestic aspects of Canada's anti-terror program. My idea was to probe — and hopefully to illuminate — this asymmetry. Unless I could deal with both parts of the Canadian response, my theme could not be adequately expressed.

In the result, I now acknowledge, with deep gratitude, the "go ahead" that my CCLA colleagues gave me. At the same time, I state unequivocally that, while my comments on Canada's domestic anti-terror program will likely reflect the consensus in the organization, no such characterization can be made with respect to the international aspect of what follows. For these purposes, I write as an individual and not as the organization's representative.

This is also the point publicly to convey my thanks to the Donner Canadian Foundation for a generous grant to the Canadian Civil Liberties Education Trust, CCLA's research and educational arm. As a result of this grant, I was able to spend the effort and obtain the assistance that were needed to produce what follows.

As usual, I was helped by many people. I am deeply grateful to the following who read and commented insightfully on various aspects of the manuscript: Sydney Goldenberg, Marv Schiff, Dawn Clarke, Cyril Levitt, Ken Swan, Owen Shime, Louis Greenspan, and John McCamus. Goldenberg, Swan, and McCamus read, re-read, and commented on certain revised sections. John McCamus came up with, what I believe is, the rather clever title for the book.

I note, with thanks, the contributions of my CCLA staff colleagues and volunteers: Alexi Wood, Noa Mendelsohn-Aviv, Josh Paterson, Jeremy Patrick, Ben Aberant, Laura Swan, and Danielle McLaughlin. I also extend my thanks to the staff for the way they kept up the activities of the organization while I was immersed in writing. As for Donna Gilmour, my administrative assistant, I continue to marvel at the efficiency and speed with which she typed the manuscript and its many revisions.

It is appropriate, at this point, to express my gratitude to the Honourable Anne McLellan, Canada's former deputy prime minister. Despite many attempts, my colleagues and I were unable to find the sources for certain quotes attributed to her. I do believe that I had seen the quotes, but I did not keep them and could not find where I saw them. Ms. McLellan knew me to be a critic of many of her policies. Nevertheless, she graciously acknowledged the ownership of the quotes in question. Despite whatever criticisms I continue to make about this country, I am proud of the civilized nature of much of the discourse that occurs here. And I am pleased to note that my interaction with Anne McLellan falls squarely within this category.

I also extend a special word of thanks to Motek Sherman, student-at-law with CCLA. His prodigious and tenacious research was responsible for producing the notes appended to the manuscript. Within a relatively short period, he found the sources for the quotations that appear here. This involved a Herculean effort. Motek simply would not let any obstacle interfere with the effort. His contribution is especially noteworthy because he harboured a number of significant disagreements with the views I was expressing. Obviously, this represented performance well beyond the call of duty.

Last but not least, my thanks to the folks at The Dundurn Group, my publisher: Kirk Howard, Beth Bruder, and my editor Michael Carroll. They were warm, welcoming, and helpful. Although it goes without saying, I will say it, anyway: those who helped me, bear no responsibility for what I have written. Whatever criticism is evoked belongs to me alone.

A. Alan Borovoy
Toronto, Ontario
June 2006

Preface

This book is dedicated to the memory of North America's tough-minded democratic Left.

The tough-minded democratic Left of North America is becoming an endangered species. I am referring to the kind of people who, just a few years ago, played a vital role in North American political life. My heroes combined a compassionate social conscience with a keen sense of reality. In Canada I am referring to the likes of social democratic leader David Lewis and labour leaders such as Dennis McDermott, Eamon Park, and Terry Meagher. In the United States, this constituency included politicians such as Democratic Party senators Henry "Scoop" Jackson, Hubert Humphrey, and Paul Douglas, as well as socialist icon Norman Thomas and civil-rights leader Bayard Rustin. Among the intellectuals who exhibited this kind of thinking were John Dewey, Sidney Hook, and Irving Howe.

A few examples will most effectively illustrate what it is that made the contributions of these people so valuable. In the case of the Canadians, these leaders fought to promote greater economic security and equality for workers, racial minorities, women, and the poor. They also championed the cause of civil liberties. In the latter connection, consider, for instance, how courageously David Lewis challenged the propriety of the Canadian government's

1970 invocation of the War Measures Act. With the whole country applauding that action taken by then Prime Minister Pierre Trudeau, Lewis made an eloquent case for the opposition.

At the same time, however, these leaders were clear-headed and realistic about the dangers posed by other elements on the Left. Lewis, McDermott, Park, and Meagher were in the forefront of the battle to divest the totalitarian Communist Party of any significant influence within the ranks of organized labour. This sophistication also led them to resist a number of left-wing efforts aimed at promoting Canada's withdrawal from the North Atlantic Treaty Organisation (NATO). Since Dennis McDermott lived longer than most of the others, he had occasion to speak out against the anti-Israel direction of a number of Canada's current labour leaders. Despite his opposition to the then right-wing policies of Israel's Ariel Sharon government, McDermott believed in the paramount importance of defending the democratic Jewish state against the threat of Palestinian terror.

As for those American leaders, they promoted the cause of civil rights for blacks and the creation of a viable welfare state. On the issue of civil liberties, they were outspoken opponents of the notorious Senator Joseph McCarthy. At the same time, every one of them supported the goal of U.S. policy: to prevent the spread of Soviet Communism.

In some situations, this position produced unexpected outcomes. In the late 1940s, for example, socialist leader Norman Thomas denounced presidential "peace" candidate Henry Wallace because of the latter's "apologies for Soviet cruelty and bad faith." Much later, socialist intellectual Irving Howe similarly chewed out left-leaning author Lillian Hellman because of the way she had belittled the harm caused by the Communist Party. In the 1970s, New Deal liberal Senator Scoop Jackson criticized conservative U.S. President Richard Nixon for the *softness* of Nixon's détente policy towards the Soviet Union. In the 1980s, self-styled social democrat Sidney Hook chastised right-wing U.S. President Ronald Reagan for being too "irresolute" in his opposition to Soviet expansion.

Of course, these people did not constitute a monolith. They had a number of disagreements even with one another. Nor am I suggesting that each of them would support all of the positions I espouse. But what is important about them is the similarity in their basic orientation. This is best understood in terms of the pathologies to which certain extremes of the Right and the Left are particularly susceptible. I summarized them in an aphorism a few years ago: "The pathology of the Right is a hard heart. The pathology of the Left is a soft head."

What distinguished the people to whom I have referred is their refreshing combination of soft heart and hard head. For all their idealism in promoting their left-of-centre philosophies, they had no illusions about the extremists on *their* Left. At a time when terrorists and their rogue-state sponsors are threatening the very survival of our precious democracy, and at a time when our side is under increasing pressure itself to abandon the principles of democracy, we urgently need the kind of contribution these people made. If ever there was a time for political resurrection, this is it.

A Beginning Word

The atrocities of 9/11 have reinforced a central message of history: as long as authoritarians anywhere in the world have resources or power, democracies are not likely to be left in peace.

In the twentieth century, the democracies faced threats to their very survival. First it was Nazism, a particularly malevolent manifestation of fascism. Then it was Communism, a particularly cynical bastardization of socialism. Nazism appealed to humankind's worst proclivities: racism and xenophobia. By contrast, Communism exploited the best in us: the yearning for social justice and equality. Through activities such as the Holocaust, the Nazis fulfilled their malevolent promise. Through activities such as the Gulag, the Communists betrayed their benevolent promise. Both represented a mortal challenge to democracy.

The terrorists of the twenty-first century are closer to the fascists of the twentieth century. There is, however, one crucial difference: a large component of today's terrorism is fanatically religious. Al-Qaeda, the major terrorist organization, contends that many of its activities are directed by God Himself. As a consequence, such terrorists are a particularly formidable enemy.

What makes al-Qaeda so important in this regard is that, according to the most authoritative sources we have, it is the organization that perpetrated the massacres of 9/11. That operation combined a high level of political ingenuity, technological efficiency, and sheer human cruelty. Al-Qaeda's recognized leader is Saudi-born Osama bin Laden. From numbers of interviews he has given and announcements he has made, we acquire a glimpse of what this enemy is all about.

Many wrongdoers go out of their way to deny — and even to conceal — their misdeeds. Not Osama bin Laden. He has openly boasted that "we are terrorists." He has said, "Yes, we kill their innocents."[1] Indeed, bin Laden has said of the Americans: "We do not have to differentiate between military or civilian. As far as we are concerned, they are all targets."[2]

Bin Laden's xenophobia appears as unshakable as it is frightening. According to him, Muslims "should sever any relations with the Jews and the Christians … whoever befriends Jews and Christians becomes like them, and becomes one of them in their religion and in their infidelity."[3] Indeed, bin Laden has proclaimed that "killing Jews is top priority"[4] and that "judgment day shall not come until the Muslim fights the Jew."[5] According to him, the enemy is "the crusader alliance led by America, Britain, and Israel … a crusader-Jewish alliance."[6]

Western leaders who have ordered their soldiers into war have nevertheless described the exercise as a regrettable necessity. Israel's Golda Meir, for example, once expressed this feeling with particular eloquence. The one thing, according to her, that Israelis could not forgive is that the Arabs made the Israelis kill them. Contrast that sentiment with the comments of Osama bin Laden on the occasion of the suicide bombing of the American ship USS *Cole*: "The pieces of the bodies of infidels were flying like dust particles. If you could have seen it with your own eyes, you would have been very pleased, and your heart would have been filled with joy."[7] And in relation to the fear in America engendered by 9/11, bin Laden reportedly exclaimed, "Thank God."[8]

And what are bin Laden and his cohorts attempting to achieve? Perhaps a helpful source of information in this regard is one of his religious mentors, the blind sheik Omar Abdel-Rahman, who was implicated in the 1993 bombing of the U.S. World Trade Center.

The aim, according to the sheik, is to "conquer the land of the infidels."[9] One expert, Yossef Bodansky, has described bin Laden's ultimate goal as "world domination by the kind of Islamic radicalism we see in the Taliban Afghanistan regime or in Sudan or in Iran."[10] Bin Laden himself seemed to corroborate at least part of this analysis when he made the following statement: "As for the Taliban, we pray to God to keep their feet firm, and guide them on the right path. In our opinion, their positions are firm, right, and principled."[11]

It will be remembered that, in the Taliban's Afghanistan, girls were not allowed to attend school, men were required to wear beards, and certain convicted felons had their limbs chopped off in front of large public gatherings.

Bin Laden has implied that such an Islamic regime is the outcome he seeks for the United States itself. Upon being asked what his organization wanted from that country, his "letter to the American people," dated November 24, 2002, replied as follows: "The first thing that we are calling you to is Islam.... It is to this religion that we call you; the seal of all the previous religions."[12]

Although the Nazis and the Communists also sought domination, they were essentially secular movements. This band of terrorists, however, is thoroughly theocratic. Osama bin Laden contends that "God ... ordered us to carry out jihad."[13] He maintains that on 9/11 the pilots of the hijacked planes were "blessed by Allah."[14] As for nuclear arms, he says that "it would be a sin for Muslims not to try to possess"[15] such weapons. He considers "hostility towards America" to be "a religious duty."[16]

Bin Laden's theology also provides an alluring incentive for himself and his followers. He talks freely about the rewards that Muslims can look forward to "in God's paradise."[17] He also thunders that "little is the comfort of this life, as compared with the hereafter."[18] He points out that his youthful followers "only want one thing, to kill so that they can go to paradise."[19] As far as he is concerned, to be "killed for Allah's cause is a great honour ... something we wish for."[20]

How is it possible to negotiate with people like that? What could we possibly offer them that would rival "God's paradise"?

Nor could our armed might and willingness to use it serve as a deterrent to those who welcome death "in Allah's cause." Such considerations are what likely compelled Yossef Bodansky to declare these terrorists "will stop only when their ultimate goal is achieved or they are all dead."[21]

To further their objectives, these and other contemporary terrorists have committed one massacre after another. Their avowed victims have included not only able-bodied adults, but also vulnerable children. Indeed, their recent litany of activities has involved even the use of children as suicide bombers. In this connection, note the slogan of one such terrorist group: "The children are the holy martyrs of tomorrow."[22]

Having been made aware of the devastation that terrorists such as al-Qaeda are prepared deliberately to inflict on innocent people including children, we have every reason to believe that no horror is beyond them. If they should ever acquire nuclear, biological, or chemical weapons, I fear for the suffering that people in the West will be made to endure. It is obvious that Western leaders must spare no effort to deny these terrorists possession of such weapons.

An aggravating factor in today's world is the existence of unscrupulous rogue regimes that, in varying degrees, have sponsored, financed, and even armed such terrorist entities. These nations have included Iran, Syria, Saudi Arabia, and Libya. Together with North Korea, Iran is becoming a mortal threat in its own right. The combination of such countries and terrorist organizations makes the world of today appear more dangerous than it did even at the height of the Cold War.

Although terrorism had struck on many previous occasions, 9/11 represented a special case. It was one of the rare times since the American Revolution that an alien power had hit the continental United States. And it was a hit of major proportions: a wanton slaughter of several thousand non-combatant civilians. The experience created the look and feel of vulnerability in the world's only superpower. This paradox traumatized large numbers of people in North America.

Even before the dust had quite settled, our society was deluged with analyses, proposals, appraisals, and advice. We were counselled to go on a war footing, suspend civil liberties, undertake mammoth aid programs to address "root causes," treat such terrorism as nothing unusual, and immerse ourselves in perpetual prayer.

Unfortunately, there was no dearth of foolishness in the advice we received. In some ways, this foolishness was one of the most important responses to the events of 9/11. In democracies, public policy is heavily influenced sooner or later by the state of public opinion. To the extent that fallacious analysis and argument dominate the political marketplace, the options effectively available to government are limited accordingly. Such limitations are likely to spawn dubious policies. And in a number of ways they did.

Now that a few years have passed since 9/11 occurred, it might prove helpful to revisit some of the more questionable things that have been said and done. After all, fallacies do not correct *themselves*. We who have experienced them must identify and dissect them. Unless we do, those fallacies are likely to be repeated again and again. And so will the flawed policies that result from them. I intend to focus, therefore, on the factors — and fallacies — that appear to have influenced public opinion and the public response to them.

Since 9/11 there has been much activity both abroad and at home. Canada joined the American incursion in Afghanistan and refused to participate in Iraq. This country also responded to the deepening conflict between the Arab countries and Israel in the Middle East. At home Canada enacted a host of special anti-terror measures that could jeopardize the state of our domestic civil liberties. Not the least of the latter threats are those that could particularly affect innocent Canadians of Arab origin and Muslim religion.

Unlike other societies, those professing to believe in democracy must be especially concerned with the ethical components of the policies they adopt. Our governments are mandated to protect our people and institutions from harm. Terrorist attacks can inflict irreparable injury on both. Thus, the very survival of our democracy requires that we vigorously resist what the terrorists are trying to achieve. At the same time, we must not forget the democratic values we are trying to preserve. It is essential that the anti-terror measures we adopt cause no more damage than necessary to our democratic principles.

I profess no special expertise in foreign policy, international relations, national security, or law enforcement. But along with many others I believe I am quite capable of detecting fallacious arguments and flawed analyses about such matters, especially in regard to their ethical components. This then is what the ensuing discussion is about. It is an inquiry into the fallacies that have characterized public commentary about the ethical validity of Canada's post-9/11 policies both abroad and at home. I propose to examine the quality of analysis that has emanated from Canadian politicians, opinion leaders, media commentators, and authors. At various points, this will include a look at foreign material that is particularly influential in Canada.

In order to create a framework for what is coming, it might help for the reader to know that, ethically, I believe Canada has adopted too many restraints abroad and too few at home. It is in this sense that I see our response as "categorically incorrect." In my view, it would have been ethically better for Canada to be more inhibited in the domestic arena and less so in the international arena. In the words of the vernacular, we got it essentially "ass backwards."

Yet the identification of such fallacies should not be read as conclusions about policies. As for involvement abroad, I largely avoid conclusions because for that a number of strategic factors must be addressed that are beyond my field and outside the scope of this inquiry. Take the war in Iraq, for example. Virtually every day there are new allegations that cast doubt on exactly what were — and are — the true state of the facts. I am in no position to get to the bottom of this apparent mess. Yet I continue to believe that whatever explanations may ultimately emerge, we can and should examine the quality of the debate, particularly what preceded the invasion — and some of what occurred afterwards. Hence, I consider it critically important to root out the fallacies that have afflicted our public discourse. Hopefully, such an exercise will help us to prepare for tomorrow's challenges.

As for the measures at home, I reach more conclusions because for that the relative strategic factors are closer to my general field and the ensuing analysis takes more of them into account. After all, the balance between safety and freedom is the daily meat of my organization, the Canadian Civil Liberties Association.

In any event, my objectives here will be amply fulfilled if the reader agrees that certain kinds of reasoning represent an inappropriate way to evaluate public policy.

A number of the issues that illustrate themes here have evolved and others have emerged since this writing was essentially concluded. There has been no attempt to stay on top of the daily news. But, to whatever extent I am able to catch such changes, acknowledgement will appear in the notes rather than in the text.

At this point, it might be helpful to elucidate a little bit more on the major premise of my position. My views have been heavily influenced by the barbarism of the twentieth century — Nazism, fascism, Communism, genocide, and apartheid. If humankind has learned anything from the horrors of the past one hundred years, it is that the one hope there is for humanity is democracy.

Democracy is the only system in this world that puts a premium on human dignity. Even though people differ in all kinds of ways, for example, in ethnicity, proclivity, and even ability, the democratic system considers them equal in *dignity*. Democracy is also the only system in which the central decisions are made not by the forced coercion of the bullet, but by the free consensus of the ballot. In this regard, the twentieth century has demonstrated time and again that injustices are less likely to endure — or even to emerge — in an atmosphere of free public debate culminating in fair and free elections.

For such reasons, I contend that the legitimate goal of our country's behaviour abroad and at home is the preservation of democracy. This is the lens through which our policies should be detected, dissected, and amended. In consequence, it will also be the basis for the comments I will be making here.

PART ONE

Abroad

I

In General

THE "ROOT CAUSES" PHENOMENON

How often have the Western democracies been admonished to address the "root causes" of terrorism? Since 9/11, perhaps no single theme has been repeated as frequently by America's critics. It is not without significance that this challenge has been expressed by certain elements on the Right as well as on the Left and by those of a religious as well as by those of a secular persuasion.

Within less than a week of the attack on the World Trade Center and the Pentagon, Christian Right leader Jerry Falwell effectively pinned the blame on the opponents of school prayer, abortion advocates, gays, lesbians, and feminists. He warned that "God will not be mocked ..."[1] Lacking Mr. Falwell's pipeline to the Almighty, the vast majority of North Americans will be unable to grasp how the atrocities of 9/11 could have been prevented by keeping women in the home and homosexuals in the closet. More to the point, however, is Reverend Falwell telling us that, by reverting to greater discrimination against these groups, we can stop terrorism?

On the secular Left, linguistics professor Noam Chomsky also urged us to examine the root causes. In his view, however, those causes and their solution took on a somewhat different form. "If we devote our resources to ... addressing the roots of the 'campaigns of hatred,' we cannot only reduce the threats we face but also live up to the ideals that we profess."[2]

Jim Selby of the Alberta Federation of Labour, also from the secular Left, was even more definitive: "Unless you address the core, root issues of terrorism ... that is global poverty, inequality — then we're not going to solve anything."[3]

Another partisan of the "root causes" approach is South Africa's much-admired Bishop Desmond Tutu. He has warned that "we will never win the war against terrorism as long as there are conditions that make people desperate and, therefore ... vulnerable to being recruited and used by unscrupulous people." According to Tutu, "until we win the war against poverty, disease, ignorance ... we are really playing marbles."[4]

The portrait of the terrorist suggested by these comments is one of a lumpen proletarian living in dire poverty and despair. After all, these commentators would probably insist, who else but those living without hope would be prepared to kill *themselves* for a cause? But this theory happens to collide with certain realities. Consider the suicide killers of 9/11. In the main, they were educated middle-class professionals.[5] They were not living anywhere close to poverty or despair.

More systematic research seems to corroborate such observations. In a recent study of the subject, Harvard professor Alberto Abadie was unable to find "a significant association between terrorism and ... income."[6] My purpose in mentioning these facts is not to oppose the waging of a vigorous fight against poverty wherever it may exist. It is simply to register the caution that the war on poverty cannot be seen as a panacea for the war on terrorism.

Toronto Star columnist Linda McQuaig has another view about root causes. According to her, "terrorism is actually a response to military interventions perpetrated by Western governments."[7] On the basis of this theory, she says, "some solutions may be possible." For example, "we should carefully scrutinize what actions our governments are up to in the Middle East, to assess whether these actions are justified and, if not, to stop them."[8] Presumably, such an approach would both improve our foreign policy *and* reduce the risks of terrorist attack. After all, according to her, what so many of these attacks have in common is the goal of compelling the Western "democracies to withdraw military forces from territory that the terrorists consider to be their homeland."[9]

One problem with McQuaig's analysis arises from the difficulty in determining precisely what lands the radical Islamists have in mind when they demand Western departure. At one time or another, representatives of this militant movement have talked as though they have proprietary interests in many countries beyond the Middle East such as Indonesia and the Philippines. But even Europe is not exempt from their claims. Despite the fact that Andalusia in southern Spain was "de-Muslimized" a few centuries ago, radical Islamists continue to express both anger at what occurred and a yearning to restore the status quo ante. McQuaig is obliged to tell us exactly what territory is appropriate for the accommodation of the terrorists' demands.

In any event, her proposed solution does not appear to square with what bin Laden himself said he wanted from the United States. As indicated, his earlier cited letter to the American people said, "the *first* thing that we are calling you to is Islam [emphasis added]."[10] Thus, religious conversion would appear to rank high among his priorities. Nor does the "second thing" in bin Laden's letter address Western evacuation of alleged Muslim territory. Among other matters, the "second thing" calls upon the United States "to reject the immoral acts of fornication, homosexuality, intoxicants, gamblings, and trading with interest."[11] This part of his letter went on to admonish the Americans for choosing "to invent your own laws as you ... desire ... rather than ruling by the Sharia of Allah."

For these purposes, is there any reason why Osama bin Laden should not be taken at his word? While his letter did go on, at a later point, to promote the departure of U.S. forces from Muslim lands, he nevertheless seemed to regard America's alleged irreligiosity as a central issue.

27

This impression is reinforced by the writings of Sayyid Qutb, one of militant Islam's leading ideologists. In the opinion of this Islamic scholar, the source of much evil in the contemporary world is the Western idea of a secular society in which there is a separation of church and state. Qutb has been described by the U.S. scholar Paul Berman as being afraid that "liberal doctrines about religion would spread from the Western societies into the Muslim world, and take root there, and crowd out Islam."[12] This description would help to illuminate bin Laden's apparent obsession with how America governs *itself.*

In view of her thesis, McQuaig might also have a hard time explaining why the terrorist cell that staged the train bombings in Madrid continued to plan attacks against Spain even after that country's new government had decided to withdraw its troops from Iraq.[13] Thus, Jonathan Freedland in the *Manchester Guardian* expressed the essence of al-Qaeda's objectives as the "reintroduction of the caliphate, an Islamic state governed by Sharia law ..."[14] Anyone purporting to tell us what these terrorists really want, at the very least, must deal with these questions.

Of course, we should always scrutinize the actions of our governments, as McQuaig suggests, "to assess whether [they] are justified and, if not, to stop them." But why, she must tell us, should we believe that this would be likely to cut much ice with the extremists of al-Qaeda? Still, there is no sensible way to hitch our foreign policy wagon to the various demands of the terrorist horse. Should Great Britain have considered surrendering Salman Rushdie to Iran in order to accommodate the Ayatollah Khomeini when he issued a fatwa on the author's life? And what about the fate of Israel? For al-Qaeda, this matter is not simply a dispute over territory but rather opposition to the very existence of the Jewish state. It would be obscene for any of the Western democracies to even contemplate renouncing their support of Israel for the sake of placating a group of terrorists.

Admittedly, McQuaig did not suggest we make any changes that were not otherwise justified. Her mistake, however, was to encourage the accommodation of Islamic interests as a possible way to shield ourselves from terrorist attack. We should do the right thing whether or not it pleases the proponents of radical Islam. But the path proposed by Linda McQuaig contains the lure of appeasement. We would be wise to be wary.

✦

In the spring of 2002, the United Church of Canada weighed in on Arab-Israeli tensions by declaring that it "deplores all acts of terrorism." This statement, of course, is incontestable. But the church decided to go further and pronounce on the root causes of the problems between these two peoples. After all, to whatever extent causes can be identified, solutions might be found. In the following comment, the church articulated the conclusion of its analysis: "While feeling deeply for Israeli victims, and passionately for the continued security and well-being of Israel, the United Church nevertheless strongly states that at the root of the violence and instability of the region is Israel's illegal occupation of Palestinian territories."[15]

This perspective has been expressed by numerous other commentators. Consider *Globe and Mail* columnist Rick Salutin. Anyone wanting to destroy a commitment to terror, Salutin warned, "must destroy the conditions that engender it." In his view, "the root of the current trouble … is not the right of Israel to exist, but its right to expand, settle, and control for 35 years."[16]

There is something curiously ahistorical in this analysis. What do these commentators believe occurred *before* the inception of the 1967 Israeli occupation? That period was also marked by scores of terrorist incidents and by two outright wars between Israelis and Arabs. Before 1967 not a single neighbouring Arab country recognized the State of Israel. Those who so blithely blame the Israeli occupation for the current woes are ethically obliged to explain why, in light of the conflict preceding 1967, they have chosen the events of 1967 as the root cause of the trouble.

While the United Church came up with its one-sided declaration, the Anglican Church aimed for a particle of additional equity. In the course of doing so, however, the Anglicans appear to have wound up saying virtually nothing: "When Israel withdraws from its illegal occupation of Palestine, when Palestinians are free to return to their homeland, when civilians are no longer the targets of terror, either from suicide bombers or government tanks, then healing will begin."[17]

In short, when all parties behave differently from the way they are now behaving, there might be peace. One of my professors labelled such observations "a penetrating glimpse into the obvious." Not satisfied with its tautological contribution to the debate, the Anglican Church went on to insist that "any other path will simply entrench violence and death as the norm for this generation and many generations to come."[18] Unless the parties opt for peace, there will be violence and death. For such insight, the world and posterity must be truly grateful.

Another problem with these "root cause" theories is that they are usually employed to bolster the argument for avoiding military conflict. It was in the context of the proposed invasion of Iraq that Bishop Tutu made the statements cited above. In the course of invoking the objective of looking for root causes, such commentators have been known to misstate the point of the exercise. *Globe and Mail* columnist Rick Salutin, for example, declared that the "bombing of Afghanistan did not destroy al-Qaeda the way an emphasis on black ops, bribery, assassination, etc. might have."[19]

But this was not the purpose of the American operation in Afghanistan; no one operation could have hoped to accomplish the destruction of al-Qaeda. The idea was to remove the Taliban regime, a key source of support and sustenance for terrorism in that region and elsewhere. The most that Salutin's proposed surgical incursions would likely have achieved was the removal of a few al-Qaeda operatives. Important operatives perhaps, but not important or numerous enough to have decimated the entire organization.

Admittedly, the much larger and more open campaign that the United States actually conducted in Afghanistan had to increase the risk of attracting more recruits to the al-Qaeda cause.

But leaving the Taliban regime in place would *also* have compounded this risk. Salutin's criticisms failed to address the multidimensional character of the dilemma involved.

In any event, why should support for any military mission require that it completely defeat al-Qaeda in particular or terrorism in general? Why would it not suffice for a military engagement simply to make a *significant contribution* to such overall purposes? Of course, no single battle or even series of battles will completely annihilate terrorism. The same would likely be true of social and economic aid programs.

Further to the statement quoted above, Bishop Tutu also warned that we "will not get true security from the barrel of a gun."[20] This statement is certainly true. But even if the barrel of a gun cannot give us "true security," it would probably give us a hell of a lot more security than we would have without it. In such ways, a number of commentators have provided questionable advice for the war on terrorism. It is hard to understand why our response to terror must be so restricted. There appears to be no valid reason why we cannot — and should not — embrace a multi-level strategy, one that entails covert operations along with social, economic, political, *and* military initiatives.

THE PERPETUAL PARAMOUNTCY OF PEACE

As long ago as October 2001, the British Columbia Teachers' Federation expressed a much-acclaimed theme when it declared that "we go to war because we are misled or fail to use our intelligence to avoid it."[21] This sentiment, appearing as it did when war in Afghanistan was being contemplated, is even more fallacious than it is popular. The statement effectively implies that war could *never* be preferable to all of the available alternatives. It effectively implies that there is *always* a preferable alternative.

On this basis, Britain should never have militarily challenged Adolf Hitler. What was the preferable alternative then? Unless the B.C. Teachers' Federation is sitting on the best-kept

31

secret in history, the *only* alternative then available was the Nazi engulfment of all Europe — and then perhaps more. The necessary implication is that it is always wise to avoid military resistance to aggressive dictators. How far does this mean, in turn, that it is always better to live life on your knees than to risk death on your feet?

To whatever extent the B.C. teachers would wish to avoid the enslavement of the democracies by any dictatorships, they must also avoid publicizing their sentiments about war. Otherwise, aggressive dictators would have no incentive to make any deals whatever with the democracies. If they knew in advance that the democracies would *always* prefer any option to war, the dictators could simply choose the path of intransigence. They could demand what they want, convinced they would get it because of their knowledge that we would not fight to prevent it. It is disconcerting, indeed, to realize that such foolishness is being disseminated as wisdom by so important a constituency in our society.

DEFERENCE TO THE UNITED NATIONS

One of the most curious notions that has been invoked time and again in the war against terrorism — as it was before — is the attribution of superior legitimacy to the decrees and decisions of the United Nations (U.N.). By contrast, much of the unilateral action undertaken by democratic countries such as the United States and Israel is considered devoid of such legitimacy.

Both before and during the military campaign in Afghanistan, the then federal New Democratic Party (NDP) leader Alexa McDonough insisted that "the U.N. must ... lead in the campaign against terrorism."[22] In a speech to the House of Commons, she said that it is NDP policy "to oppose offensive military intervention that is not sanctioned by the United Nations."[23]

Writing in the *Globe and Mail* at the inception of the 2001 military action in Afghanistan, legal scholar Michael Mandel contended that "since the United States and Britain have undertaken this attack without the explicit authorization of the [U.N.] Security Council, those who die from it will be the victims of a crime against humanity, just like the victims of the September 11 attacks."[24]

The United Nations' subsequent authorization of the Anglo-American operation appears to have made all the difference in the world to Bill Graham, Canada's then foreign minister. Since he criticized the Israelis for their military incursion into the West Bank after a number of suicide bombings, a reporter pressed him as to why he did not similarly criticize the Americans in Afghanistan. Graham replied, "The U.S. and Canada went into Afghanistan with explicit U.N. Security Council approval after September 11. Israel didn't have that. The U.N. has demanded that Israel withdraw."[25]

Similar comments have been made in the context of the debates over the invasion of Iraq. During these debates, the *Toronto Star* insisted that "the lawful way runs through the U.N., not the Washington beltway."[26] Acknowledging the validity of pressing Iraq to mend some of its unacceptable ways, *Star* columnist Haroon Siddiqui added this key qualification: "But who would judge, the United Nations or the United States?"[27] Siddiqui's colleague, another *Star* columnist, James Travers, talked about how important it was "to establish the U.N., not the U.S., as the arbiter of international order …"[28]

In light of how often the media bombarded the public with such sentiments, it was not surprising to find Canada's then prime minister, Jean Chrétien, insisting that any action against Iraq would have to be done under the auspices of the United Nations. When U.S. President George W. Bush finally took the American case against Iraq to the U.N. Security Council, the *Toronto Star*'s eminent foreign affairs columnist, Richard Gwyn, talked about the contest between "power and legitimacy."[29] The assumption, of course, is that the United States embodied the former and the United Nations the latter.

The philosophical rationale for this deference to the United Nations has been expressed by some of those who have been in the front lines of international diplomacy. In urging restraint regarding the then prospective war against Iraq, Lloyd Axworthy, Canada's former minister of foreign affairs, declared, "better we should act to preserve an international system based on a *rule of law* than to become a cheerleader for a precipitous act ... [emphasis added]"[30] Similarly, Axworthy's successor, Bill Graham, warned that, if any nation is in violation of U.N. rules, "we are there to enforce the rules, not something else."[31] And according to no less a practitioner of international diplomacy than U.N. Secretary-General Kofi Annan, "every government committed to the rule of law at home must be committed to the rule of law abroad."[32]

To be sure, the rule of law represents the very heart of the democratic system of justice. It is the principle that protects us from the arbitrary whims of those with power. Committed democrats must strive, therefore, to promote the rule of law as widely as possible. It should be our objective to ensure that no people are condemned to live without it.

Unfortunately, there is a large discrepancy between what we might seek and what happens to exist. Underlying all of these entreaties to prioritize the role of the United Nations is a fallacious assumption: that the United Nations, in fact, embodies the rule of law. This contention represents a gross misconception of the way the world body operates.

At its essence, the rule of law requires a separation between legislative and judicial decision-making. By enacting statutes, the legislative authority formulates the standards that are supposed to govern our behaviour. This dynamic is an acknowledged political, even partisan, exercise that depends upon the relative strength of various constituencies. But the role of applying those standards to specific cases belongs to a judicial authority that has been denuded as much as possible of political interests. In that way, the system tries to ensure that no citizens will be deprived of liberty or property unless the adjudication is as objective and impartial as possible.

The United Nations does not even pretend to be governed by such principles. Its decisions are not necessarily based on principle; indeed, they are most often ad-hoc and self-interested. It is not possible to remotely suggest that the deliberations of the U.N. Security Council represent an objective attempt to apply some pre-existing law to a live situation. Thus, France and Russia were often expected to side with Iraq not because of the objective merits of any given dispute involving Iraq, but because France and Russia had substantial dealings with that country.[33]

As noted by international law scholar Ed Morgan, Security Council decisions are not "made on any basis other than the subjective interests of the voting states."[34] There is no pretense that anything more lofty is involved.

Nor are the nations with most of the power in the Security Council necessarily democracies. All of the permanent members have the power to veto actions of the Security Council. At least one of the permanent members, the People's Republic of China, is a ruthless and repressive dictatorship. And although Russia has made strides in the direction of becoming a democracy, it still has a long way to go. Indeed, Russia has recently reversed course. Why then should we so blithely assume that the decisions made in such an undemocratic way by non-democrats are entitled to more reverence and respect than those made separately by member governments that are accountable through democratic processes to democratic electorates?

This is not to disparage completely the value of the United Nations. The world body performs a number of valuable functions, including humanitarian services and peaceful mediations. My quarrel here is addressed to those who would empower the United Nations to veto the ability of democratic member governments to protect their various interests in the international arena.

There is, in my view, an overriding issue that should be assessed in determining the ethical propriety of a state's international behaviour: to what extent does a proposed action serve the interests of making the world safe (or safer) for democratic institutions? For democrats this concern should be paramount. The experience of the twentieth century has demonstrated again and again what measures tyrants and terrorists are prepared to adopt in order to undermine — or even overthrow — the democracies.

Those wishing to ensure the survival of democratic institutions must address developments abroad as well as at home.

For these reasons, it is appropriate to evaluate international behaviour according to its likely impact on the survivability of democratic self-government. And there is no legitimate reason to require that decisions serving such interests should be subject to vetting by the U.N. Security Council, that is by those whose conduct is serving diametrically opposed — or even different — interests. In short, it is simply unconscionable to insist that the right of any democracy to defend its democratic institutions requires approval — to use Charles Krauthammer's colourful epithet — from the butchers of Tiananmen Square.

THE MULTILATERAL REQUIREMENT

It has also been argued that there is something inherently and morally wrong with the willingness of countries such as the United States to undertake unilateral military actions against other nations. Unquestionably, the multilateral route is preferable. It is strategically and tactically more advantageous.

Quite apart from the fact that other nations did join the United States in its invasion of Iraq, it would have been helpful for the Americans to have had the assistance of large countries such as France, Germany, and Russia. Their involvement could have helped to reduce the military and economic drain of both the war and the nation-building exercise that followed it. Such multilateralism would also have contributed to the appearance of legitimacy, a factor that could have made the subsequent presence of American troops in Iraq look less like an occupation than a liberation.

But these are tactical, not ethical considerations. One of the recurring Canadian fallacies in the debates over Iraq concerns the idea that unilateralism is necessarily less *ethical* than multilateralism. Consider the comments made by University of Toronto professor John Polanyi on receiving an international peace award: "we should not intervene without a convincing international

36

consensus, or we lack the necessary moral authority. We can claim that our reasons for intervening are cogent, but if we are unable to make the case to others, they are not."[35]

This is a remarkable doctrine. Suppose, during the 1930s, Winston Churchill had been the *prime minister* of Britain rather than simply a protesting Member of Parliament. Suppose he had been able to persuade the British Parliament and people that they should use military force against Hitler's mid-1930s occupation of the Rhineland. But suppose also that Britain would have been unable to convince France or any other country to join in the effort. According to Polanyi's statement, unilateral resistance by Britain would have been immoral. Yet in the opinion of eminent historians, such resistance could well have succeeded in toppling Hitler's Nazi regime.[36]

I grant, of course, that no one can predict the future with certainty. Clairvoyance is not one of the traits to which humans can lay claim. And I grant also that unilateralism carries with it risks of imperialism. But as the foregoing example should demonstrate, the *failure* to act unilaterally is also accompanied by risks. In the case of the Rhineland, the failure to act helped to cement one of the most murderous regimes in human history.

Thus, it would be the height of foolishness to bind ourselves to the kind of absolutist doctrine advocated by Polanyi and many others. While it may well be advantageous to act in a multilateral way, it could be disastrous to insist upon it. Hence, there is no substitute for evaluating the merits of all the challenges we face, free of such dogmas.

THE DOCTRINE OF PRE-EMPTION

South Africa's Bishop Desmond Tutu expressed a widely shared view when he condemned the U.S. plan to invade Iraq as an unacceptable "pre-emptive" action. "Is this a principle that is of universal application?" Bishop Tutu asked. "Or is it something that applies only to the U.S. because they are the only superpower?"[37]

When it is fleshed out, this critique effectively portrays the United States itself as a rogue power. The *Toronto Star*'s Richard Gwyn says the American doctrine of pre-emptive defence "is a fancy way of saying the U.S. will do what it pleases whenever it pleases."[38] Gwyn's fellow columnist, James Travers, talked about the "deeply troubling U.S. doctrine of pre-emptive strikes against states it alone defines as rogue."[39]

Not only is this George W. Bush doctrine seen as an exercise in American imperialism, but according to some, it also threatens to create a dangerous precedent for others. Writing in the *Globe and Mail*, Kimon Valaskakis warned that an American attack on Iraq "will set an important precedent, one sure to be invoked by potential imitators." The following are some examples of the kind of situation Valaskakis believes could be triggered by such American action: "Under this doctrine, Pakistan could perceive a clear and present danger from India and attack first, or vice versa. Israel and the Arab states could use the same logic of quick first strikes; for that matter Iraq could launch a pre-emptive strike against the United States, on the legitimate pretext that it perceives a clear and imminent threat from the latter."[40]

Quoting South Africa's Nelson Mandela, Richard Gwyn expressed a similar theme when he warned about "every nation copying the U.S. by doing their own thing whenever they can get away with it."[41] An advertisement published in the *New York Times* signed by a number of former generals and academics warned that "a pre-emptive strike on Iraq ... would free other countries to use military force."[42] And University of Toronto scholar Janice Stein declared that "it is foolhardy in the extreme to legitimate a principle that would grant every state a right to use military pre-emption that depends only on its subjective definition of the character of its adversaries."[43] According to Bill Graham, Canada's then foreign minister, the U.N. Charter permits pre-emptive strikes only "when it is clear that the enemy is getting ready to attack you."[44]

It is not clear whether the foregoing critiques would regard a pre-emptive strike, in the absence of an imminent attack, as *always* impermissible, or are they saying that pre-emption can be legitimated by the United Nations? If it is the former, it is no longer acceptable. If a nation can never resort to such pre-emptive strikes, it would become effectively helpless against today's weapons of mass destruction. As spelled out by U.S. President Bush, these weapons can be "easily concealed, delivered covertly, and used without warning."[45] To require a threatened nation to wait until an attack is imminent is effectively to confine tomorrow's victims to the doctrine of *posthumous* self-defence.

Does such pre-emption then become permissible only if approved by the U.N. Security Council? As indicated earlier, a restriction of this kind would mean that the right of any democracy to protect itself in this way would require the approval of one of the world's most repressive dictatorships — the People's Republic of China. For obvious reasons this, too, must be unacceptable.

Then what about the danger that a pre-emptive attack by the United States will somehow legitimate similar action by others? Does such U.S. action mean that all hell is likely to break loose throughout the world? These predictions appear to be based on the questionable proposition that, in general, the other nations of the world are currently restrained by respect for one another's sovereignty, international law, and/or reverence for the United Nations.

This, of course, is sheer fantasy. These restraints are not self-enforcing. On the contrary, in the context of the international jungle, nations are restrained by the disapproval of their citizens, the anticipated damage their adversaries will inflict on them, and/or by the power of the United States. Despite the many aggressions that have occurred since the creation of the United Nations, the world body has only acted twice to reverse such an aggression — 1950 in Korea and 1991 in Kuwait. And both times the exercise was made viable by the leadership of the United States. Again there is no reason to believe that this situation would be altered one whit with or without the American invasion of Iraq.

EQUIVALENCE MONGERING

A related and recurring fallacy is one I like to call "equivalence mongering," the insistence on equating aggression by autocracies with the protection of democracies. In this connection, *Toronto Star* columnist Linda McQuaig has provided a juicy example:

> The United States alone has 9,000 nuclear warheads....
> By contrast, Saddam doesn't even have one ... if
> Baghdad's appetite [for weapons of mass destruction] is
> unquenchable, how could one characterize Washington's?
> ... [I]t doesn't seem particularly surprising that Saddam
> seeks weapons of mass destruction. He'd have to be some
> kind of peacenik — or just a guy with a death wish —
> not to be scrambling to assemble some heavy-duty
> weapons, given the long-standing, open hostility of
> Washington....[46]

Thus, according to McQuaig, America's nuclear capacity and Iraq's nuclear ambitions were ethical equivalents. To her it doesn't appear to matter that the nukes at Washington's disposal must defend the survival of democratic institutions while those Iraq sought to acquire would destroy those institutions. Moreover, McQuaig justified Saddam Hussein's quest for "heavy-duty weapons" on the basis of America's record of hostility towards him. But that hostility began when Saddam invaded Kuwait. Prior to that there was no such hostility. Are we obliged, therefore, to view Hitler's increased animosity towards Western Europe as an appropriate outgrowth of Allied resistance to his conquest of Poland? By resisting his attack on Poland, did Britain and France not demonstrate their "long-standing hostility"?

The *Toronto Star*'s Thomas Walkom was apparently determined not to be outdone by his colleague. Consider his equivalence mongering:

The bad news is that a more serious threat [than terrorism] … has emerged. That threat, perhaps not so ironically, is the United States itself.…

Americans look at Iraq and see an aggressive country run by a ruthless dictator who … wants to develop nuclear bombs.

The rest of the world looks at America and sees a country historically far more aggressive than Iraq ... one that not only possesses, but has actually used nuclear weapons.[47]

With these statements, Walkom surpassed McQuaig. For the sake of argument, let us assume the United States has, in fact, been "historically far more aggressive than Iraq." Must the current administration of George W. Bush be held accountable for the history that preceded it? The same holds, of course, with respect to the actual use of nuclear weapons. The administration of Harry S. Truman made that fateful decision in 1945. Must the administration of George W. Bush in 2002 answer for it? By contrast, Iraq's aggressions that America was challenging were actually committed by Saddam Hussein, the ruler in power when Walkom made his statement. While Saddam didn't use nuclear weapons — he didn't have any — he did use other weapons of mass destruction and killed hundreds of thousands of innocent Iranian and Kurdish civilians with them.

Remember, too, that when the United States used nuclear weapons it was attempting feverishly to end, not to start, a terrible war with Japan. While the pros and cons of that pivotal decision have been debated endlessly over the years, it should not be forgotten that the United States did not initiate hostilities; it was responding to them. Saddam, on the other hand, was the aggressor in Kuwait, Iran, and Kurdistan. This is not to pass judgment on the American atom bombing of Hiroshima and Nagasaki; it is simply to note the substantially different circumstances involved.

In any event, as indicated, the American actions to which Walkom was comparing Iraq's were committed by governments other than that of George W. Bush. Indeed, the key one was committed more than half a century earlier.

For an example drawn from an entirely different context, consider this one from Osgoode Hall law professor Michael Mandel: "Bombing of Afghanistan is the legal and moral equivalent of what was done to the Americans on September 11."[48] The 9/11 attack was designed to terrorize a functioning democracy — the United States. The bombing of Afghanistan was designed to unseat a repressive, terrorist-supporting dictatorship — the Taliban regime. The ostensible purpose of the 9/11 attack was to effectuate the removal of "infidels" from Islamic holy places in Saudi Arabia, even though Americans were there with the explicit consent of the Saudi government. The ostensible purpose of the American bombing in Afghanistan was to disrupt the terrorist network between al-Qaeda and the Taliban that had encroached on America without its consent. The 9/11 attack deliberately targeted innocent civilians; the bombing of Afghanistan attempted to minimize civilian casualties.

None of this is to endorse every detail of American foreign policy. To whatever extent the United States employs disproportionate force or incurs undue risks to innocent civilians, it would deserve criticism. My aim here is a more limited one. I am simply arguing that whatever disagreements anyone might properly have with the international behaviour of the United States, it is not to be equated with the behaviour of tyrants and terrorists.

For all of its faults, the United States remains essentially a democracy whose government derives its power from the freely given consent of the citizens it governs. None of America's rogue-state or terrorist adversaries are comparably answerable or accountable to an electorate that enjoys a large measure of freedom of speech, freedom of assembly, freedom of the press, freedom of association, and secret-ballot elections. These freedoms — admittedly imperfect and inadequate — have enabled the citizens of the United States to exert a significant influence over their government's international behaviour.

This is not to ignore the argument that the American people are subject to government and media manipulation. Such manipulation, of course, does exist, exerting fluctuating influences at different times. But it co-exists at all times with a corrective phenomenon: the essentially free and pluralistic media and their competition with one another. This competition serves to counteract the impact of manipulative behaviour. While there can be no guarantees that the truth will prevail, the constant competition creates a fighting chance that falsehoods will erode. America's adversaries have nothing remotely similar.

Nor is this to suggest that democracies necessarily behave in a just manner. To be sure, they are capable of serious immorality, as illustrated all too often by the United States itself. My point is a less ambitious one: as between democracies and other powers, there is a significantly better chance that the democracies will resist, avoid, redress, or at least reduce the perpetration of injustice. The combination of a free — and, therefore, diverse — press, open debate, and the right of citizens to protest publicly and to replace their governments are the factors that help to counteract the human propensity to behave unjustly.

Moreover, the United States is virtually the only nation in the world with the ability and the interest (potential at least) to protect the survival of democracy. By contrast, many of the tyrants and terrorists of this world are bent on destroying the democratic system. It is not necessary, therefore, to embrace everything the Americans do in order to repudiate the notion of equivalence mongering. Despite its shortcomings and excesses, the power of the United States provides the best, perhaps the only, hope there is for a world in which democratic institutions can survive. For these purposes, I paraphrase a comment that was once made during a Canadian federal election campaign: don't compare the United States to the Almighty, compare it to the alternatives.

PART ONE

RETALIATING, NEGOTIATING, AND
ACCOMMODATING

In the summer of 2001 — before September 11 — the Israelis retaliated, as they have periodically, to the recurring bouts of terrorism *they* have been suffering. They attacked a building in the West Bank city of Nablus that was owned and operated by the terrorist group Hamas. In the course of the attack, the Israelis assassinated their targets, a couple of skilled bomb makers, but they also killed a handful of apparently innocent civilians. Although the Israelis quickly apologized for what they had done to the innocent victims, they were denounced by the European Union and Amnesty International.[49]

It is clear that the Israelis had not intended to kill the innocent civilians. If they were being criticized for not taking adequate care in that regard, there might be a legitimate issue. But the comments of Amnesty International included a criticism of the decision to kill the bomb makers. Of course, there might be legitimate questions about the tactical wisdom of the Israelis trying to go after their enemies in this way. But the Amnesty rebuke included a *moral* dimension: "In these state assassinations, the Israelis offer no proof of guilt, no right to defence."[50]

In my view, there would indeed be a moral problem with carrying out such a deed in a place that had a viable and enforceable rule of law. My commitment to the rule of law requires presumptive deference to it wherever and whenever it operates. I see no reason, however, for such deference in the context of a repressive dictatorship or a political vacuum. You would have had to turn Yasser Arafat's West Bank upside down to find anything remotely resembling a viable rule of law. Should Israel have attempted to serve subpoenas? Can you imagine the Palestinian authorities holding the impugned suspects for longer than an hour?

In the absence of more information, I am unable to comment on the extent to which the Israeli action created unwarranted risks to innocent people. Subject to such considerations, I do not believe there is an ethical problem with the targeted assassination

44

of those reasonably believed to be terrorists in the setting of a dictatorship or a vacuum where the rule of law cannot viably function. Nor is it legitimate to assert any equation between the deliberate targeting of those reasonably believed to be guilty and those unquestionably known to be innocent.

While Israel itself has been careful to articulate limits on the permissibility of its retaliatory tactics, some of its supporters have adopted less admirable postures. In this regard, the *National Post* reprinted an article by retired U.S. Army officer Ralph Peters that originally appeared in the *Wall Street Journal.* He was commenting on the 2002 midsummer Israeli killing of a Hamas leader on the West Bank. The deed was executed by way of a missile that the Israelis fired at their target's residence, a multiple dwelling that housed his family and a number of others. About a dozen Palestinian civilians died in the blast. According to Peters, "the world must learn that, when civilians allow terrorists to use them, the civilians become legitimate military targets."[51]

Of course, Peters's conclusion is not controversial. Those who consciously help terrorists are fair targets themselves. It is not believable, however, that all those who perished in this raid were willing accomplices. Surely, the *children* who died in the attack cannot be categorized in this way. Supporters of Israel can claim no legitimacy for their cause by invoking shameless fictions.

Peters may be standing on firmer ground with his argument that those who are fighting terrorists are entitled to pursue them even when they hide "amid the civilian population ..."[52] Unless this could be done, many terrorist acts could be committed with complete impunity. It is nevertheless morally obligatory for democratic anti-terrorists to keep civilian casualties as low as possible. Thus, it is fair to ask whether the Israelis needed to attack that person in that way on that night. After all, a missile fired at a dwelling in the middle of the night is very likely to create civilian casualties. The Israelis are duty bound to explain why no alternate courses of action were adequate in the circumstances.

Of course, the idea, as much as possible, is to avoid the situations that keep producing the recurring bouts of terrorism and retaliation. This aspiration raises the issue of negotiations. If only the parties to any of these conflicts could find some way to reconcile their differences through peaceful negotiations! Here, too, the public debate has included some fallacious advice. The *Globe and Mail*'s Rick Salutin has advised those involved in the Middle Eastern conflict to assume "that most people on both sides want peace, will compromise and will respond to a decent offer, because they would rather live than die. This would not solve everything, but it would leave the haters and killers on each side increasingly isolated."[53]

Even assuming the reasonableness of the assumptions that Salutin makes about "most people on both sides," the problem is that, as far as the Palestinian side was concerned, it likely would not have mattered as much. While Israel was a vibrant democracy where the citizens were entitled to raise hell about government policies, no comparable description can validly apply to the situation that was then under the Palestinian Authority. Remember, Salutin made this statement when Yasser Arafat was alive and in power.

Imagine what would have happened to any Palestinians in the West Bank who participated in a strong demonstration calling for Arafat to crack down on the terrorists of Hamas or Islamic Jihad! I am not suggesting that the Arafat regime was immune to any and all internal protest action. Nor am I ignoring the periodic criticisms voiced by certain Palestinian intellectuals. But I am suggesting that vehement action *against terror* would have been an incomparably risky exercise. Thus, even though Arafat periodically denounced terrorism himself, he could not be counted on to protect anti-terror protesters from the wrath of terrorists.

On the other hand, all kinds of Israelis — from the Left, Right, and Centre — have openly and vigorously protested the policies of whatever government exercised power in Israel. Thus, while the majority of Israelis who want peace can influence their government, not enough of their counterparts on the Palestinian side were able to do likewise. For this reason, Salutin's admonition was not particularly helpful.

When the Israelis announced in the spring of 2002 that they would no longer deal with Arafat, they sparked another round of fallacious criticism. According to Rick Salutin, "the notion that [Arafat] exerts total control over young people willing to die is ludicrous."[54] Similarly, Haroon Siddiqui stated that "Arafat can no more control the violence than Sharon can provide the security he promised the Israelis."[55]

I find it hard to appreciate how these observations illuminate the issues. If Arafat could but wouldn't control the acts of terror, the Israelis were obviously right to repudiate him. But why should it make any difference if Arafat could not control the violence? In such an event, there would still be no point in dealing with him. In this world, you negotiate with those who can deliver. Otherwise, we might just as well insist that the Israelis negotiate with the proverbial first twenty names in the telephone directory of any randomly chosen city.

The Israeli response to this apparent inability to find reliable negotiating partners was to build a fence along the border between the Israeli and Palestinian populations. By making it difficult for the suicide bombers to cross over into the Jewish state, the Israelis hoped that the fence would significantly reduce the incidents of terror.

In an early August 2003 column published in the *National Post*, Charles Krauthammer sharply rebuked the U.S. State Department for proposing that the United States get tough with Israel unless the Jewish state stops building the contentious barrier. According to Krauthammer, this U.S. tactic made "the fence the issue, rather than the terrorism that made the fence necessary."[56] To bolster his argument, Krauthammer noted that the United States has built stretches of fence along the Mexican border to prevent foreigners from coming in to take jobs. In his view, "it takes a lot of audacity to demand that Israel stop building a fence whose purpose is to prevent foreigners from coming in to commit mass murder."[57]

As Krauthammer expresses the argument, it evokes an airtight resonance. Nowhere in his column, however, did he mention the most significant problem that the fence poses for the prospects of fair play in Israeli-Palestinian relations. For these purposes, the issue is not *that* the fence was being built but rather *where* it was being built. The Israelis were reportedly building virtually all of the fence on Palestinian property.[58] There has been no comparable suggestion that any parts of the American fence were built on land belonging to Mexico.

Numbers of Palestinians have complained that the fence is dividing their land so that they are losing significant portions of it. Others complain that they might have to pass through Israeli checkpoints to go from one part of their land to another. There are also allegations that the fence effectively blocks access to schools, places of employment, and health facilities.

It may be that Krauthammer can answer these arguments. In any event, he did the Israeli cause little service by ignoring them in the way he did. There appear to be compelling reasons for the Israelis to build the fence. As much as possible, however, the fence should avoid any needless interference with the daily lives of the Palestinian people. It is not without significance that the Israeli Supreme Court acknowledged these inequities and ordered the Israeli government to make some relocation changes.[59] This constitutes another example of how certain Western supporters of Israel are less sensitive to these ethical imperatives than are key components of Israeli society itself.

DEMOCRACY AND SOVEREIGNTY

Another fallacy committed by commentators on the Middle East arose in the late spring of 2002. U.S. President Bush at long last called for democratic processes in the territory under the jurisdiction of the Palestinian Authority.[60] But to the consternation of many he added that the United States was not prepared to deal with Yasser Arafat even if the Palestinians were to elect him democratically. According to Rick Salutin, this policy was tantamount to requiring the Palestinians "to democratically elect someone the U.S.

approves of."[61] Here Salutin was quoting with approval Canada's then foreign minister, Bill Graham, who said "where I find inconsistency is the insistence that a democratic process be put in place but then that democratic process will be pre-determined."[62]

In my view, Graham and Salutin are finding inconsistencies where there are none. I would have thought that freedom of association is a two-way street. I defend your right to associate with or elect whomever you please. But if you associate with or elect someone threatening to my interests or values, I will not associate with you. Why can't all of these rights co-exist? While insisting that the Palestinians enjoy democratic rights, President Bush believes the Americans should also be able to retain theirs.

It is necessary at this point to address a fallacy in connection with democracies initiating military action against dictatorships. The fallacy to which I refer is the homage that many commentators insist that we unreservedly pay to the autonomy and self-determination of the nations with which we co-exist in this world. But as far as dictatorial regimes are concerned, exactly whose autonomy is involved? Certainly, the *people* who live under such regimes can hardly experience anything resembling self-determination. And to whatever extent dictators abuse their people, the experience of autonomy would be even less.

Very often the commentators who admonish us to respect self-determination also question by what right we presume to judge either the quality or even the existence of such rights in other countries. Unfortunately, there is no adequately objective way we or anyone else can make such judgments. As indicated earlier, this role is not one that can be validly played by the United Nations. Unless we are prepared simply to stand by and watch the peoples of other nations suffer, we have no choice but to make the best judgments we can under whatever circumstances obtain.

Alternatively, even if we were to believe that we must not presume to decide for other people what is good for them, we can surely decide what is good for *us*. On this basis, a number of U.S. policy-makers have concluded that peace in the Middle East — and, therefore, in the world — requires the democratization of the Arab nations. According to these policy-makers, the one hope there is for peace lies in the unwillingness of the Arab masses to continue living, and suffering, in the current state of war. But without democratization those masses will be powerless to make the necessary changes in the behaviour of their governments. Hence, the adoption of a policy that would, by force if necessary, bring the opportunity for democracy to the countries of the Middle East.

I do not claim sufficient expertise to judge the extent to which this analysis is valid in today's Middle East. Nor do I feel competent to judge whether the affected countries *could* successfully adapt to democracy. Suffice it for my purposes here to contend that, if the facts on the ground were favourable, there would be a strong ethical argument for coercion aimed at the democratization of that region. On the other hand, even if democratization may be seen as essential, it could well not be sufficient.

I am not necessarily urging a policy of military intervention against any and all such dictatorial governments. To be sure, many issues will need to be examined in order to make such determinations. Even ethically it is necessary to engage in a cost/benefit analysis: how much damage will armed intervention cause? How does this stack up against the damage entailed by the status quo? Would pro-authoritarian extremists or pro-democratic moderates be the more probable victors in democratic elections? How soon? How lasting? What are the likely consequences, both short and long term, to the most directly affected people and the rest of the world?

To ignore such factors is to emulate the behaviour of fanatics — a posture hardly worthy of democrats. My object is simply to note that respect for the territorial integrity of other nations is not a value deserving of unqualified reverence, irrespective of how much the people there might be suffering and what other interests might be applicable.

2

On Iraq

A PERSPECTIVE

The policy surrounding the Iraq war dramatized many of the ethical fallacies that have influenced Canadian behaviour. While I am very critical of these fallacies, I repeat that the ensuing remarks should not be read as conclusions about the ultimate acceptability of the war.

In order to reach such conclusions, it would be necessary to assess a number of strategic issues that are not even addressed here. Was the war in Iraq a diversion from — or a contribution to — the war on terrorism? Should there have been less focus on Iraq and more on Iran and North Korea? To what extent are the United States and its allies able effectively to address the situations in a number of the world's theatres? If not, what trouble spots should command priority attention? What was the likely impact of the war on the short- and long-term welfare of the people in the most affected countries and around the world? What methods short of war could have achieved the legitimate goals of the Western democracies?

The resolution of such questions is essential to a comprehensive evaluation of Iraq policy. For my purposes here, however, these issues lie outside the scope of the discussion. As indicated, my interest here centres primarily on the ethical grounds that influenced commentary on policy. I respond, therefore, to the arguments of others rather than spell out a "stand-alone" thesis about the wisdom, or even the morality, of the U.S. action. The focus is on preparing ourselves to avoid ethically fallacious thinking in our *subsequent* confrontations with terrorists and their rogue-state sponsors. What more is to be done, for example, about al-Qaeda, Iran, and North Korea? Unless we discern and correct the fallacies in the Iraq situation, we could well be ill-prepared for the next crisis.

One of the problems arising from the Iraq invasion concerns the growing perception that the war was a failure. Even if this assessment were to become the Western consensus, we should guard against the mistake of concluding that the main arguments against the war were, therefore, valid. As I hope to show, some of those arguments provide a fallacious basis indeed with which to address the remaining dangers in the post-9/11 world. By the same token, the fact that some of those arguments were wrong does not make the Iraq war right.

Since there were more ethical arguments against than in favour, they occupy the thrust of my responses. I also include, however, a critique of the ethical posture assumed by several supporters of the war.

THE QUESTION OF EVIDENCE

Perhaps the most frequently invoked basis for the invasion of Iraq had to do with the belief that Iraq possessed weapons of mass destruction. Indeed, that country had actually used such weapons in its 1980s war against Iran and its early 1990s action against the Kurds. At the conclusion of the 1991 Gulf War over Kuwait, the Western allies and the United Nations adopted a number of measures designed to divest Saddam Hussein of the weapons in question. Upon being persuaded that these measures had utterly failed to achieve the desired result, the United States, the United Kingdom, and a coalition of willing nations invaded Iraq in

March 2003. The coalition did not include such important nations as France, Germany, Russia, and China. Canada also did not join in the effort. Nor did the invasion ever receive the blessings of the United Nations Security Council.

As of the date of writing, no such weapons of mass destruction have been found. Indeed, it is now believed that when the invasion occurred, Iraq simply did not have the impugned weapons. A recurring fallacy in post-war discussion has invoked the failure to find the weapons as a retroactive vindication of the critics' original arguments. But it could not have been known then that the weapons would not be found thereafter. Thus, the relevant question is: what was it most reasonable to believe at the time the invasion occurred?

In order to justify a pre-emptive strike such as occurred in March 2003, the one advantage of requiring at least preparations for an imminent attack goes to the question of evidence. The more imminent the anticipated attack, the less need to produce evidence: by then intentions would be obvious. But where there is no particular indication of imminent attack, as was the case with Iraq, the question of evidence becomes more difficult. The result was some questionable advice.

Consider the *Toronto Star* columnist Richard Gwyn. During the lead-up to the war, he argued that, "Iraq is being required to prove a negative; namely that it does not have any weapons of mass destruction. This is a logical impossibility."[1] There was, of course, a point here. How could you prove, for example, that you have never been to China? On this basis, Gwyn contended that the United States and United Nations "have an obligation to do everything to meet the standard of reasonable evidence...."[2]

As valid as such points might be in other contexts, they were not applicable here. The United States and the United Nations had no onus whatsoever. They did not have to prove that Saddam had weapons of mass destruction; in those circumstances, the onus was on *him*. By the time the earlier contingent of U.N. weapons inspectors left Iraq in 1998, they had revealed a disquieting situation: the regime of Saddam Hussein had failed to account for *tons* of biological and chemical weapons that the inspectors knew it had recently possessed.[3] What then had happened to those weapons? Their whereabouts were within Iraq's exclusive knowledge. Not surprisingly, therefore, Saddam was pressured to undertake expressly that he would account for their location and disposition.

On April 6, 1991, Iraq "accepted ... the provisions of Security Council Resolution 687" that had been adopted three days earlier.[4] According to that resolution, Iraq was to transmit to the U.N. secretary-general "a declaration of the locations, amounts and types" of all of its "chemical and biological weapons."[5] Yet, as of November 8, 2002, the U.N. Security Council adopted Resolution 1441 "deploring the fact that Iraq has not provided an accurate, full, final, and complete disclosure ... of all aspects of its programs" concerning its "weapons of mass destruction."[6] Thus, for more than a decade, Saddam Hussein was in violation of the international community, several U.N. Security Council resolutions, and his own explicit undertakings. And as of the date of writing, this violation has never been rectified.

Yes, I know that in late 2002, Saddam's government made available a declaration of several thousand pages purporting to document the whereabouts of the contested weapons. But according to the then U.N. chief weapons inspector, the dovish Hans Blix, this material "is rich in volume but poor in new information about weapons issues."[7] Pointing out that "only declarations supported by evidence will give confidence about the elimination of weapons," Blix concluded that "in this respect we have not so far made progress."[8]

During the 1990s, Iraq was frequently caught cheating about its possession of these weapons.[9] Its response led to the removal of the 1990s regime of U.N. weapons inspectors. In view of the kind of government we were dealing with, what was most reasonable to believe in 2003 — that, in the absence of any inspection, Saddam had given up these weapons, or that he was working feverishly to increase them? Put this way, there can be little question: it was most reasonable to believe that, at the crucial times, the taboo weapons were in the possession of Saddam Hussein. This belief was also reportedly held by the major intelligence agencies of the world, including those of the United States (during the administrations of both George W. Bush *and* Bill Clinton), Britain, France, Germany, and Russia.[10] Moreover, the U.N. weapons inspectors who left Iraq in the late 1990s had verified Saddam's possession of these weapons during the 1990s.

This is why the logic of the situation validated the relevant resolutions and undertakings: Saddam Hussein was duty bound to account. His failure in this regard emerged, therefore, as a key ethical factor justifying action against him.

Some critics have contended that U.S. President George W. Bush knew all along the weapons weren't there. If this claim turns out to be validated, Bush will deserve the harshest of criticisms and much more. But unless *we* knew or should have known that such allegations against Iraq were false, it would have been folly for us to oppose the war on such grounds.

This point is critical. The intriguing feature of so much of the opposition to the war is that it was *not* based on doubts that Iraq had weapons of mass destruction. Key voices spoke against American policy, even though they believed that Saddam Hussein did have the crucial weapons. Consider Edward M. Kennedy, the liberal U.S. senator from Massachusetts. In September 2002, he said, "we have known for many years that Saddam Hussein is seeking and developing weapons of mass destruction."[11] Yet only a few weeks later the same Senator Kennedy voted *against* authorizing the Iraq war.[12]

Similarly, not many of the Canadians who spoke against the war did so on the basis that Iraq was devoid of such weapons. This tendency created a fundamental problem. A substantial number of commentators, Canadian and American, were influenced by regrettable fallacies. Regardless of whatever facts ultimately emerge as to Iraq's putative possession of the weapons in question and regardless of what other arguments there are for and against the war, these fallacies represent dangerous grounds for public assessment of foreign policy in the age of terror. This flawed approach must change if our precious democratic system is to have adequate hope for survival. I turn now to these additional fallacies.

INVASION ISSUES

A *Toronto Star* poll published in mid-September 2002 found that 44 percent of Canadians were opposed to their country becoming involved in America's planned war against Iraq. By comparison, only 38 percent favoured joining the proposed American effort.[13] In view of a subsequently published poll, this result is hardly shocking: in the later poll, while 56 percent of Canadians said that Saddam Hussein posed a greater threat to world peace than did George W. Bush, as many as 38 percent fingered the U.S. president.[14]

Perhaps this political orientation north of the Forty-ninth Parallel owes something to the kind of material that has been published in the Canadian press. Statements by opinion-makers and columnists have expressed a wide variety of misgivings about America and its intentions. This exercise is fair enough, but some of these commentators have committed significant fallacies.

In late September 2002, the *Toronto Star*'s Haroon Siddiqui reproduced some remarks made by South Africa's Bishop Desmond Tutu regarding America's planned invasion of Iraq: "We know that it is going to [mean] many civilian casualties. If the loss of civilian lives is reprehensible in New York and at the Pentagon and in Pennsylvania, how is it not equally reprehensible when it happens in Iraq or in Iran or in Afghanistan?"[15]

Again this comment expressed a fair concern. To be sure, it was reasonable to expect an American invasion of Iraq to produce many civilian casualties. But what this column by Siddiqui neglected to add was any assessment of likely casualties if the invasion did *not* occur. In the hands of Saddam Hussein, the weapons of mass destruction — it was reasonably believed he had — could pose a terrible threat to countless innocent civilians throughout the Middle East and perhaps even beyond. On the basis of both his maniacal ambition and demonstrated sadism, there was at least a reasonable basis to believe that Saddam would have used such weapons repeatedly in order to control his own citizens and to dominate his neighbours. It is not enough, therefore, to engage in such a one-dimensional analysis of any policy. It is essential to consider *all* aspects of the problem.

Another factor that very likely influenced the state of Canadian public opinion was the amount of material that impugned the suspected motivations behind American policy. In this connection, note again Siddiqui's comments in the *Toronto Star*: "[Bush's] new-found concern for the Iraqi and Iranian victims of Saddam's chemical weapons has not credence, given that America supplied Saddam with the initial shipments in the 1980s, and Washington stayed mum when he did use them...."[16]

Even more sinister motives were attributed to the United States by one of the world's greatest living heroes, South Africa's Nelson Mandela. He talked about "George W. Bush's desire to please the arms and oil industries in the United States."[17] This comment was reproduced in one of Siddiqui's columns. In a similar vein, the *Toronto Star's* Richard Gwyn argued that, even though North Korea had admitted having weapons of mass destruction, the United States preferred to focus its energies on Iraq. Why? One reason, according to Gwyn, is that North Korea "has no oil ..."[18]

The *Toronto Star's* Linda McQuaig lamented how "little knowledge" Americans have "of brutal U.S. foreign interventions." She blamed this shortcoming on the U.S. media for portraying "U.S. actions abroad as well-meaning efforts to bring democracy to other parts of the world, rather than aggressive attempts to advance U.S. economic and political power."[19] To the *Toronto Star's* Richard Gwyn, however, the "action against Saddam [was] just a side issue." According to him, "America ... intends to keep [its] military strength beyond challenges.... No Carthage will be allowed to arise to challenge today's Rome."[20] In short, the real aim of U.S. foreign policy, in Gwyn's opinion, is to ensure American hegemony in perpetuity.

Despite these speculations about the true motives behind American policy, Gwyn could not restrain himself from attempting a psychological diagnosis. In his view, George W. Bush was moved by "an overpowering need." Gwyn said "it's not military or political ... but personal. Bush needs to save his Daddy's face for not having done in Saddam a decade ago." In this regard, we can be grateful to Gwyn for avoiding the jargon of psychology. He summed up this analysis by describing Bush's policy on Iraq as "the behaviour of a fruitcake."[21]

It is not clear from the above what importance each of these commentators attached to motivation. The question that must be addressed, however, is what difference does motivation make? It all depends upon the purpose of the exercise. For the purpose of predicting the behaviour of certain countries, for example, motivation can matter. But when it comes to assessing the merits of their policies, motivation is irrelevant. Suppose, for the sake of argument, that the comments quoted above were all valid descriptions of what the United States was trying to achieve. Where would that have gotten the critics of America's policy on Iraq? Was it not possible that America was doing the right thing for the wrong reasons?

At the time of World War II, a number of Marxists contended that the primary motive of the Allied powers was to preserve capitalistic markets, not democratic freedoms. Even if that were so, it would still have been morally legitimate to fight Hitler. Regardless of possible profiteering motives, the war against Hitler served to protect democratic institutions. Thus, the war deserved the support of those who believe in democracy. The test of a policy does not depend upon the motives of those who conceive it. It depends upon the merits of its likely impact.

Thus, even if President Bush was primarily concerned about oil, his nation's place in the world, or his father's place in history, our support for — or opposition to — his policy in Iraq should be influenced by the extent to which that policy was needed to make the world adequately safe for democracy. And we would be morally obliged to apply this test even if we were to conclude that

George W. Bush, in his heart of hearts, never gave a sweet damn about the survival of democratic institutions.

Before leaving the subject of America's possible motivations, I feel the need to address the idea that the goal of American hegemony may be driving the Bush policy. In today's world, American power might well be the most reliable guarantor of democratic institutions. Again this is not necessarily to endorse every American position. It is simply to recognize that the United States is probably the only nation that can effectively resist the challenges posed by tyrants and terrorists. No other nation appears to have sufficient power for the job and, as indicated earlier, the structure of the United Nations is too flawed. Whatever differences we might have with George W. Bush on any number of matters, therefore, he cannot be legitimately faulted for trying to ensure his country's continued pre-eminence.

A theme that became particularly popular in Canada during the period before the invasion of Iraq was the idea that there were viable alternatives to fighting such a war. To whatever extent this was true, of course, the morality of the invasion would have been rightly condemned. After all, it is not ethically acceptable to shed blood when there are less-disastrous alternatives capable of achieving whatever legitimate interests are at issue. The alternative to war that especially appealed to numbers of Canadians was the U.N. inspections system that Saddam Hussein permitted to operate in Iraq from late 2002 on.

In early February 2003, the *Toronto Star*'s Linda McQuaig announced that this inspection system was "working so well that we should consider imposing it on other countries."[22] In support of this encouraging conclusion, McQuaig cited three factors: the fact that the inspectors were on the job, the fact that they were being given unfettered access, and the fact that nobody in Iraq was threatening to kick them out.

These factors were certainly evidence of an ongoing U.N. effort to disarm Iraq. But they were hardly evidence that Iraq was, in fact, being disarmed. Although the chief inspector, Hans Blix, pleaded for more time, his reports nevertheless repeatedly noted that large quantities of lethal material remained "unaccounted for."[23] In view of the tons of chemical and biological weapons that had been documented during the 1990s, the periodic destruction of such a weapon from time to time was not worth crowing about.

Approximately a month before the war in Iraq began, former Liberal solicitor general Warren Allmand, former Conservative minister of external affairs Flora MacDonald, and former NDP leader Ed Broadbent published an article in the *Globe and Mail* contending that "the inspectors must be allowed time to complete the task of ensuring that all possible weapons of mass destruction have been eliminated."[24] As impressive as this tri-partisan appeal may have been, it failed to address the key impediment the inspectors were facing: the non-cooperation of Saddam Hussein. True, he let the inspectors roam around freely and he periodically relinquished certain weapons. But as indicated earlier, the onus was on him. He was obliged to come clean. Yet, as of the March 2003 inspectors' report, he had not accounted, as promised, for tons of dangerous weapons he had recently possessed.

As Charles Krauthammer wrote, "it is impossible to find weapons of mass destruction in an uncooperative country."[25] Even assuming that this statement exaggerates reality, the ability to find such weapons under these conditions would be, at the very least, extremely difficult. Thus, it wasn't enough to urge, as the tri-partisan appeal did, that the inspection system be improved. What needed improving was the behaviour of the Iraq government. Without military action, what reason was there to believe that the requisite improvement would be forthcoming?

Other commentators urged more time for the inspections in the hope that this would increase the likelihood that important countries such as France and Germany would join the coalition.[26] As helpful as the involvement of such nations would have been, how realistic was it to expect such a development? After all, those countries had lucrative financial dealings with Iraq. In any event, Saddam Hussein had been playing games with the Western allies for more than twelve years. Thus, there was no ethical imperative for postponing Saddam's day of reckoning when the onus all along remained with *him*.

In some ways, perhaps there is an even more critical drawback with the proposal to give the inspectors more time. What would have constituted the end of the inspections system? The most the inspectors could ever have said is that they had tried everything they could and had failed to find the weapons. But such a disclosure would *not* have been tantamount to a confirmation that the weapons did not exist. In light of Saddam's record, there would still have been an arguable need for confirmation. And this would have required the very accounting that he had been failing to provide. Thus, without more comprehensive accounting by Iraq, the state of the inspection regime could not furnish an ethically compelling basis for further delay.

Another alternative to war was recommended by the *Globe and Mail*'s Rick Salutin. His quest for other remedies impelled him to suggest "indicting Saddam at the international Criminal Court ..."[27] When I read this recommendation, I could only ask myself, "Why didn't I think of that?" Of course, we can well imagine how the threat of an unenforceable indictment would have unnerved the cold-blooded murderer of thousands of people. I am driven to offer Salutin the standard advice in such situations: don't give up your day job.

On a number of occasions, America's militancy towards Iraq was compared with its reticence about North Korea. After all, it was pointed out, North Korea already had nuclear weapons; therefore, it was already the threat that Iraq hoped to become. It is noteworthy that these critics almost never proposed curing the discrepancy by advocating military action against North Korea.

There are other differences between the two situations that could logically justify both American policies. A military engagement with North Korea would likely produce a host of worse consequences than any comparable action against Iraq. With its tough military army of more than a million, it was alleged that North Korea could probably swamp South Korea virtually overnight. Moreover, the South Korean capital of Seoul is said to be within easy range of North Korean artillery.[28] And Japan, as well, could be a convenient target.

In order to resist such possibilities, the United States would likely need to deploy much larger forces, thereby creating a risk of substantial casualties — much more than was anticipated or even sustained in Iraq. The only alternative might be to resort to nuclear weapons. Either scenario is a nightmare to contemplate. While no war would be devoid of pain, there was no reason to expect anything comparable from an Iraq campaign.

But even if the United States could legitimately be seen as inconsistent, that was no reason to oppose its action in Iraq. Such apparent inconsistency engages the kind of ad hominem that was discussed earlier in the context of motivation. Unacceptable motives and inconsistent policies cannot suffice to resolve the validity of any particular policy proposal. Each one must still be assessed on its own merits.

A major criticism of the American-led invasion focused on its unilateral and pre-emptive character. Earlier I discussed the arguments for requiring approval by the U.N. Security Council or at least the participation of a more broadly based multilateral coalition. Although there was also an earlier discussion of pre-emption, an additional comment might be warranted in the context of Iraq.

The periodic willingness to undertake pre-emptive action responds to one of the important lessons inherent in the 9/11 experience. The aim of today's terrorists — and often their rogue-state sponsors — is to inflict as much damage as possible, as suddenly as possible, on innocent civilians. The modern weapons of mass destruction are the ingredients that can fulfill this depraved ambition. In the current era, therefore, it could well be effectively suicidal for any democracies to insist that military action on their part requires an imminent attack against them. Such a restriction is tantamount to what I have labelled the doctrine of "posthumous self-defence."

I am not minimizing here the dangers of pre-emptive action. All too easily such a policy can be used to advance the most imperialistic of agendas. Without question those nations that would pre-emptively intervene in other nations must be subjected to the most exacting scrutiny. But in this dangerous world of rogue states and weapons of mass destruction, situations could well arise in which the *failure* to move pre-emptively could be even more dangerous than doing so. Unfortunately, there are no simple tests or ready-made formulae that can be invoked to resolve these issues when they arise. There is no substitute for a careful value-balancing, risk-weighing analysis as challenges occur.

✦

The critics of the Iraq war had no monopoly on fallacious arguments. Consider the following: a few days after hostilities in Iraq had begun, Paul Cellucci, the then U.S. ambassador to Canada, chastised this country for its failure to support the American effort:

> There is no security threat to Canada that the United States would not be ready, willing, and able to help with. There would be no debate. There would be no hesitation. We would be there for Canada, part of our family. That is why so many in the United States are disappointed and upset that Canada is not fully supporting us now.[29]

The anticipated reciprocity of "family" relations is not a sufficiently compelling reason for any nation, especially a democracy, to go to war. You don't kill people because of family expectations. You kill them only when there is an overriding moral or strategic need to do so.

Similarly, Margaret Wente, the *Globe and Mail*'s always interesting columnist, employed a curious argument when she noted that thoughtful Americans were puzzled by the fact that, once the war began, Canadians "haven't come onside."[30] The implication of this point is that, even if there are moral and strategic reasons not to fight, we are obliged to fight once the war begins. Even more curious is Wente's point that the Americans had the support of some forty governments representing a billion people "that includes the Anglosphere — except for us."[31] The least persuasive reason I can think of for engaging in battle is that it has become the Anglo-Saxon thing to do.

According to Rick Anderson in the *Toronto Star*, George W. Bush had ample reason to invade Iraq without relying on the "still-unproven allegations" concerning Saddam's weapons of mass destruction.[32] Anderson's list of justifications included human-rights abuses as well as Saddam's brutalization of his own citizens. What Anderson did not address was why the Americans should not, therefore, attack all the other dictatorships that have perpetrated cruelty on their own people. What about Iran, North Korea, Libya, Saudi Arabia, Nigeria, China, and Cuba? Why should Iraq be singled out simply on human-rights grounds?

Quite apart from any question of ethical restraints against democracies militarily toppling certain dictatorships, there would certainly be *prudential* inhibitions. A key reason that Iraq became a prudential as well as an ethical target was the apparently growing threat it arguably created to our legitimate self-interest. That is why the weapons of mass destruction became such a critical factor.

In any event, those weapons were the most oft-stated purpose of the American attack on Iraq. Even if other grounds could have justified the U.S. action, it was not ethically acceptable for George Bush to invoke them retroactively. Moreover, as indicated, Rick Anderson's reference to the "still-unproved allegations" against Saddam further muddied the waters. As indicated, our side did not have to prove his possession of these weapons; it was necessary for him to account for the whereabouts of those we knew he had had.

These explanations became especially confused in the months following the fall of Saddam Hussein and during the period leading to the 2004 U.S. presidential elections. Regrettably, President Bush himself exacerbated the confusion. On the subject of whether he would have invaded Iraq if he had known then that Saddam did not have the impugned weapons of mass destruction, Bush made the following statement: "Based on all the information we have today, I believe we were right to take action, and America is safer today with Saddam Hussein in prison. He retained the knowledge, the materials, the means, and the intent to produce weapons of mass destruction."[33]

Knowledge, means, intent? With these words, the U.S. president was essentially arguing that *in time* Saddam Hussein could have acquired the impugned weapons. But during a speech in October 2002 before the beginning of the war, Bush described the situation in much more urgent terms: "If we know Saddam Hussein has dangerous weapons today — *and we do* — does it make any sense for the world to wait to confront him as he grows even stronger and develops even more dangerous weapons? [emphasis added]"[34]

A number of Bush's neo-conservative supporters have attributed a still different position to him. Writing during late 2004 in the influential American magazine *Commentary*, its former editor Norman Podhoretz contended that all along the weapons were "by no means the only or ... even the decisive consideration for Bush ..." In Podhoretz's view, there was always a "long-range strategic rationale" and it had to do with the "democratization" of the Middle East.[35]

But even if there had been such strategic considerations, they were not the heart of the case that Bush sold to the U.S. Congress and the American people. In speech after speech, he kept emphasizing those weapons. And so did Richard Cheney, Donald Rumsfeld, Condoleezza Rice, and Colin Powell (remember Powell's speech to the U.N. Security Council?). Of particular significance in this regard is Bush's address to the American Enterprise Institute in February 2003, just a few weeks before the war began. Even at that late date, the president said, "we hope that the Iraqi regime will meet the demands of the United Nations and disarm, fully and peacefully."[36] The clear implication of this statement is that such peaceful disarmament could have averted the war — in short, the weapons were a prerequisite.

As indicated above, it was ethically impermissible for George W. Bush to talk afterwards as though the weapons of mass destruction had been anything but pivotal to the invasion. Thus, when he was confronted later with the apparent lack of such weapons, Bush should have said that, if he had had such information earlier, it might well have affected the *timing* of his plans: even if he was seeking to encourage democratization in that country, it may not have been necessary *at that point* to take military action. But since he had allegedly good grounds to believe that the weapons were there, he could plausibly have argued that the situation was more urgent. Alternatively, he could have said that he would employ non-military means to achieve his goals.

In the result, we are left with a quandary: the fact that Bush's post-war defence of his Iraq policy is indefensible does not make the policy itself unacceptable. As members of the public, it is imperative that *we* make the relevant distinctions.

Responding to Bush's acknowledgement that he had misstated some of the facts concerning Saddam's military capabilities, the *Globe and Mail*'s Norman Spector said, "I'm surprised anyone's surprised that George W. Bush didn't tell the whole truth about weapons of mass destruction."[37] In Spector's view, "a president has more freedom to fib," especially about foreign affairs. Quite apart from the unacceptable immorality of sending people into battle on the basis of misrepresentations, Spector's comments have serious foreign policy implications. In an era when pre-emptive military engagements might be increasingly necessary to protect the Western democracies, the credibility of those democracies is indispensable. Spector's cavalier dismissal of this factor is simply incomprehensible.

According to the respected Israeli newspaper *Ha'aretz*, U.S. President Bush told then Palestinian Prime Minister Abbas, "God told me to strike at al-Qaeda and I struck them, and then He instructed me to strike at Saddam which I did."[38] Fortunately, Bush did not attempt to sell his policy on the basis of his alleged conversation with the Almighty. But to whatever extent he might be allowing such "communications" to influence his judgment, he would effectively be disqualifying himself from any position of leadership within the Western democracies.

At its core, the conflict with radical Islam grows out of the certainty those militants feel about their ability to divine the

Divine Will. The Western democracies would denude themselves of their philosophical foundations if they ever based policy on the notion that they knew better what constitutes the Will of God. While many people in the West also believe they know God's Will, the greatest number of them are opposed to using violence as an instrument to enforce such beliefs. Indeed, this conviction has been the Western consensus for some time. One hopes that Bush's reported exchange with Abbas had nothing to do with American foreign policy.

POST-INVASION ISSUES

The aftermath of such an invasion generates a whole new set of ethical issues. How is the target country to be governed? And when is it appropriate for the liberating (or occupying) powers to leave? A word, therefore, about some of these issues.

Since the formal end of the war, there has been much criticism — and even some American acknowledgement — that the United States was not adequately prepared for the nation-building job that its victory required. The aftermath of the war brought problems of power blackouts, water shortages, and insurgent violence against both American soldiers and Iraqi civilians.[39] Indeed, it became clear enough that America's ability to keep the peace was nowhere as effective as its capacity to wage the war.

Once more the debate was infected with fallacious thinking. Although many of these fallacies were primarily political, I group them with the ethical fallacies because they occurred in the context of attempts by some nations to control the affairs of other nations — an exercise fraught with ethical implications. Although many of these fallacies were committed by Americans in relation to America, I include them here because of the paucity of Canadian response to them. After all, Canadians have generally been vocal about the perceived faults of the United States. But, on so many of the issues that follow, Canadian voices have been remarkably silent.

Many supporters of the Iraq invasion invoked the American experience in rebuilding both Germany and Japan at the conclusion of World War II. As for the twentieth-century-achievements in Germany and Japan, the confidence of twenty-first-century U.S. planners on Iraq was unwarranted. In the case of Germany, there happened to be remarkable indigenous leadership. The then chancellor of West Germany, Konrad Adenauer, turned out to be both competent and inspiring. In any event, this development was more a coincidence of history than a product of American planning.

In the case of Japan, the Americans got lucky again. They chose General Douglas MacArthur to oversee the transition to democracy. On the basis of his previous behaviour, there was every reason to expect that he would be a right-wing tyrant. Instead, he proved remarkably and unexpectedly receptive to the needs of the Japanese people. It seemed incongruous that this man who militarily attacked labour protesters in 1932 Washington would be promoting land reform in 1946 Japan.

It is significant that, among the critics, there was virtually no mention of America's Cold War failures to adequately address the political component of its conflict with the Soviet Union. While the United States deserves credit and gratitude for its military toughness and vigilance during this period, it made political blunders that are proving costly even to this day. An understanding of this history may help to illuminate American failures in Iraq.

During the early 1950s in Iran, for example, there is evidence that the Central Intelligence Agency (CIA) was instrumental in the *coup d'état* that successfully overthrew the government of Mohammad Mossadegh, the popular elected nationalist prime minister.[40] While Mossadegh seized the British oil fields in Iran, there was little basis to believe that he was controlled by the Soviet Union. In the wake of this coup, the highly unpopular shah, Mohammad Reza Pahlavi, was restored to power. The shah's much-hated regime, of course, paved the way for the revolution of the ayatollahs. Small wonder that this country has wound up as part of George W. Bush's "axis of evil."

Vietnam is widely seen as one of the key American failures during the Cold War. Indeed the spectre of the defeat in that country continues to haunt everything the Americans do. A key problem with the American effort there was the fact that at no time did South Vietnam have a government that commanded loyalty or controlled territory. The power holders in that country were a succession of repressive reactionaries and political clowns.

In that country, too, there appeared to be some alternatives: indigenous leaders opposed both to the autocrats in government and the Communists who were seeking to replace them. There were reformers such as moderate socialist and nationalist Dr. Phan Quang Dan and Buddhist leader Thich Tri Quang, who enjoyed substantial popularity among the Vietnamese people.[41] If such reformers had been in positions of government power, perhaps they might have been able to supply the critical missing link in the whole counter-insurrectionary effort: popular support. Instead, a number of such alternatives wound up in South Vietnamese jails — victims of government repression. Significantly, neither the supporters nor even the critics of America's Vietnamese policy paid much attention to these people.

At the time of the Bay of Pigs, the critics of American policy focused on the alleged immorality of the United States trying to overthrow the regime of Fidel Castro. In consequence, little attention was paid to the possibility that the Americans might have been helping the wrong group of Cuban rebels. The Cuban invasion force that landed at the Bay of Pigs was led by a number of right-wing hacks from the ousted and discredited regime of Fulgencio Batista.[42]

Yet there were other anti-Castro Cubans who were virtually ignored by the United States: an underground operating on the Cuban mainland and an exile force in North America led by former activists in Castro's 26th of July Movement.[43] These were democratic social reformers who had worked with Castro in the revolution to depose the corrupt Batista government. They had supported Castro's economic reforms but opposed his political embrace of totalitarian Communism. A prominent figure in this group was Manual Ray, Castro's first minister of public works. There is some indication that, despite his vehement opposition to Castro, Ray might have been considered too much of a "socialist" for the CIA.[44]

Again it was hard to find North Americans who were prepared to champion the cause of Castro's democratic opposition. Not surprisingly, little fuss was made about the savage prison terms Castro imposed on his former associates: twenty years for regional governor Huber Matos and thirty years for trade union leader David Salvador.[45] When those men went to jail, it was left to a small group of American social democrats and trade unionists to denounce what Castro had done. In the result, Castro's democratic opposition virtually disappeared into history and Castro consolidated his dictatorial hold on the country.

In the early 1960s, the people of the Dominican Republic overwhelmingly elected democratic social reformer — and anti-Communist — Juan Bosch as their president. When Bosch was subsequently deposed by a right-wing military coup, U.S. President John F. Kennedy revoked American recognition of that country's government.[46] This act of the Kennedy administration was a milestone in the Cold War history of America's relations with the Third World. Unfortunately, a mere two years later Kennedy's enlightened policy was reversed. President Lyndon B. Johnson sent the U.S. Marines into the Dominican Republic to thwart an uprising of pro-Bosch forces.[47] Once more the United States used its power against progressive democratic alternatives to Communism in the underdeveloped world.

And it happened again in Nicaragua. The United States supported the Contra movement, much of which was right wing and many of whose leaders had been involved in the discredited Anastasio Somoza government. Again it was hard to find Americans prepared to champion those Nicaraguans who were opposed to both the Communists among the governing Sandinistas and the authoritarians among the Contras. Consider, for example, Edén Pastora, a hero of the revolution against Somoza.[48] Consider also Alfonso Robelo and Arturo Cruz.[49] Like

Pastora, they played a prominent role in the anti-Somoza rebellion and in the early stages of the Sandinista government. They all fell out with their Sandinista comrades because of what they believed to be the growing Communization of the country.

For a significant period, Pastora had led a band of about 7,000 anti-Sandinista guerrilla fighters. But because of his refusal to collaborate with pro-Somoza elements among the main Contras, the CIA denied him the military aid he sought for his separate operations. There was even a report that conservative Contras, with the knowledge of American officials, planned to assassinate Pastora.[50] In any event, Pastora, Robelo, and Cruz were frozen out of the picture. The American intervention helped to ensure that the Nicaraguan conflict was waged primarily by pro-Communist elements among the Sandinistas and right-wing authoritarians among the Contras. America helped to ensure that key progressive democrats of that region were kept on the sidelines.

Whatever helpful changes may have occurred in some of these countries, the fact remains that for much of the Cold War, American involvement served dubious interests. Against the backdrop of this history, it is disconcerting to realize that the United States might again be wrong-headed or neglectful regarding the political component of its involvements. While the debate goes on as to how much of the nation-building effort in Iraq should be done unilaterally by America or multilaterally by the United Nations, too little discussion has occurred about the kind of social and economic reforms that may be necessary for the creation of democracy in such countries.

And to whatever extent there is a discussion about necessary reforms, there is a tendency to formulate questionable objectives. It is being said, for example, that the goal of the nation-building effort is to create a political democracy together with a highly capitalist economy. George W. Bush himself articulated the goals of American policy in this regard as one of building "entirely new political and economic institutions based on democracy, *market economy*, and action against terrorism [emphasis added]."[51]

Such comments create the apprehension that Bush may be aiming to make such societies resemble the one in America. It is important to remember, however, that the capitalism of the United States may not be suitable for many countries in this world. It is even respectably argued that the United States itself might benefit from further reform of its economic institutions. After all, in certain countries, market economics have been fingered as a key contributor to social hardship.

In order to protect vulnerable people, numbers of societies have found it necessary to impose various controls over economic activity. Not infrequently, they have been able to do this without eroding the integrity of politically democratic institutions. In short, there is no reason why socialist democracies cannot viably coexist, as they have, in alliances with capitalist democracies. Even in its rhetoric the United States often evinces an insensitivity to such important possibilities.

Moreover, there is some indication that the United States has not only failed to promote adequate reform, but it has also undermined the reconstruction effort. With apparent impunity, U.S. corporate interests in Iraq have reportedly obstructed — or at least neglected — repair and construction projects involving bridges, electricity, water, and health care. U.S. activity has also been identified as complicit in "demobilizing Iraqi state enterprises" that were highly experienced in their respective fields of endeavour.[52]

A key political issue to which American planning in Iraq seems to have paid inadequate attention concerns the conflicts among the Sunnis, the Shias, and the Kurds. As the United States has learned since the presumed end of the war, the conflicts among these groups could erupt into all-out civil war. As one crisis after another has threatened to undermine the American attempts at pacifying the country, it has become increasingly evident that, for all of its military prowess, the United States failed again properly to address the political component of its strategic decisions. As a result, the Americans gave every appearance of making up policies as they went along. While flexibility is often needed, it is hard for a world leader to command the confidence of other nations when its planning at the political level looks haphazard.

In the spring of 2004, America's strategic posture was wounded by a further defect in its political planning. I refer to the revelations of mistreatment inflicted upon Iraqi prisoners by American armed services personnel. Pictures were widely published in the U.S. and world media showing American soldiers standing guard over prisoners in poses of sexual degradation and humiliation. Others showed naked Iraqi prisoners looking terrified as they were apparently about to be attacked by ferocious dogs.[53]

As of the date of writing, it is not clear how far, if at all, this mistreatment was the result of orders from above. At the very least, there is reason for concern that the upper echelons of the American government may have failed to take adequate steps to avoid such misconduct. These pictures suggest a dismal lack of foresight and preparation on the part of the Bush administration — an issue warranting serious investigation. It is not as though the United States had suddenly found itself in a war against Iraq. That invasion had been contemplated for a few years. But once more the *political* component of the planning was nowhere in evidence.

There is another political factor in the American strategic posture that could seriously undermine its objectives. As indicated, an effective war on terrorism involves action at the military, political, diplomatic, and economic levels. Such action could well require increasingly more resources. Unfortunately, the United States has been attempting to further its program without discernible sacrifice from its own people. Yes, those who have enrolled in the armed services are making significant sacrifices. And so, of course, are their families. At the same time, however, there has been a sizable tax cut particularly favouring the wealthy elements of the population.

The result is an inadequately resourced war on terror, a disproportionate distribution of sacrifice from the population, and an enormous budget deficit. All of this risks the viability of America's efforts abroad and the solidarity of its support at home. Not a very impressive way to play the role of global leader.

✦

Despite, or perhaps because of, America's attempts to stabilize the situation in Iraq, much instability prevails. In addition to the issues already identified, a nasty insurgency rages on. And so has the disquieting increase in casualties, both Iraqi and American.

Notwithstanding these dangers, the Iraqis have turned out in ever-increasing numbers to participate in the votes both for their new government and for a new constitution. Most significant, many of them have done this even though they faced an increased risk of insurgency violence.

Not surprisingly, there has been a growing demand from both Americans and people in other countries for a U.S. withdrawal of military forces from that country. Some have called for a virtually immediate withdrawal; others have been urging a more phased departure according to a schedule to be established very soon. Canadian voices have joined the chorus in the form of an increase in rallies, demonstrations, articles, and essays.

Writing in the *Globe and Mail* more than a year after the cessation of formal hostilities, Naomi Klein expressed the wish that Canada would once again become "a haven for [American] war resisters."[54] She reminisced how 50,000 draft-age Americans came to Canada during the Vietnam War. In her view, "a fraction of that could break the back of [the Iraq] war." According to Klein, if Canada were once again to play the role it did, "it would mean that we were not just quietly opting out of the illegal and immoral war in Iraq. We would be helping to end it."[55]

Since the foregoing were the last words in the article, Klein omitted to address the implications of putting an "end" to the Iraq war in late 2004. Was she suggesting that it would be desirable for the United States to withdraw from Iraq at that point? Would she have been prepared to leave America's Iraqi allies and the other democratic elements in that country to the tender mercies of the terrorist insurgents? And how would an American withdrawal from Iraq at that point embolden tyrants and terrorists elsewhere in the world? What would be the impact on those who depend on the credibility of U.S. power? It is irreparably fallacious to urge such a termination of the "war" and not even address the welfare of those who could be detrimentally affected.

Those urging a unilateral and speedy withdrawal of U.S. forces from Iraq would do well to reflect on the situation in Iran. As of the date of writing, Iran's president, Mahmoud Ahmadinejad, has declared that the Holocaust never happened and that Israel should not exist.[56] What makes these remarks so disconcerting is Iran's nuclear capacity and its suspected attempts to manufacture nuclear weapons. In view of this leader's mindset and the behaviour of the ayatollahs on other issues, the prospects of a nuclear-armed Iran is a horror to envision. Not surprisingly, the Western democracies have attempted to head off such a development.

While the goal is easy, the means are difficult. As of the date of writing, the focus has been on diplomacy. But diplomacy works best when it is fortified by a credible threat of force. A successful use of such force against Iran is laden with problems as to what kind and how much would be needed. The more intense and widespread the military action, the more effective it could very well be. The *casualties*, of course, would also be greater. Moreover, military conflict with Iran might also help to unify whatever divisions there are in Iranian society, increase recruitment for terrorism, and create serious economic trouble.

The one way the West could prevail without such warfare is through its credibility. If the Iranian leadership believed that the West, in particular the United States, was able and willing to sustain the risks that incursions would create, there might be no need actually to engage in them.

This point is where Iraq becomes relevant. By launching the invasion in Iraq, America demonstrated considerable fibre. Can there be any doubt that this is the factor that produced the Libyan cooperation on disarmament, the Syrian withdrawal from Lebanon, and the steps towards democratization in Egypt? No one who has lived in the real world for longer than an hour can possibly believe that Muammar al-Gaddafi, Bashar al-Assad, and

Hosni Mubarak suddenly and spontaneously acquired virtue. The most plausible explanation for their seemingly precipitous reversals is fear of the United States. And that fear was activated by the attack on Iraq.

That is why an early U.S. withdrawal could be so dangerous. Just as the original invasion demonstrated determination, so would an untimely withdrawal reveal equivocation. An America so encumbered is not likely to produce the requisite fear among the maniacs who currently govern Iran. The probable result would be a dangerous, nuclear-armed Iran or some costly military entanglements. It is incongruous that those most vociferous in demanding an early U.S. withdrawal are the anti-war activists. But if they get their way, real hostilities (with Iran) may well become much more likely.

On the other hand, its very presence in Iraq could well leave the United States with too few armed personnel to take on Iran. Moreover, what is left has been at least somewhat bled by the Iraq ordeal. The contemplation of such developments has led to speculation that the West might be able to rely on deterrence to work with a nuclear-armed Iran the way it did with the Soviet Union. The problem is that even though the Soviets were malevolent they were rational. Not many observers, however, would accuse the Iranian regime of comparable rationality. Furthermore, a nuclear-armed Iran would pose a special threat to a democratic neighbour — Israel.

While the resolution of such matters lies beyond this inquiry, it is appropriate here to note the failure of some commentators even to mention these issues. It is fair to characterize this failure as a critical fallacy.

PART TWO

At Home

I

In General

Despite the fact that the triggering act of terrorism occurred as late in 2001 as September 11, the Parliament of Canada managed to enact more than 150 pages of complex anti-terrorist measures before the end of 2001. The government's Bill C-36 was introduced in mid-October, subjected to hearings by both the House of Commons and the Senate, amended, enacted, and proclaimed before the end of December. Among other things, the resulting law contains new powers of preventive detention and compulsory testimony, a new power to brand individuals as "terrorist groups" without convicting them of any unlawful conduct, a new prohibition against most financial dealings with such people, and a new and broad requirement to inform on people.

Commenting on the criticisms of this legislation from her former colleagues in the law schools of the country, Canada's then justice minister, Anne McLellan, declared that she "didn't sense much attempt on the part of the so-called academic community to acknowledge changes in circumstances and new realities" since the September 11 atrocities.[1] While I have not performed a comprehensive count or a scientific survey, I have noticed the frequency with which law professors have begun their critical pieces with comments about the horrors of September 11. According to David Schneiderman of the University of Toronto, "the event was simply beyond the capacity of anyone to imagine."[2] The first words appearing in a critique by Queen's University's Gary Trotter were: "The unspeakable magnitude of the September 11, 2001, terrorist attacks."[3] His colleague Don Stuart wrote similarly about "the horrifying events of September 11."[4]

Indeed, one would have to be an outright clod not to recognize the enormity of that date. It requires a special dimension of cruelty to deliberately target so many innocent people for the kind of death that was inflicted at that time. And it requires a special dimension of hatred for people like Osama bin Laden to be so willing to sacrifice his colleagues, the perpetrators, and for them to sacrifice *themselves.*

Former justice minister McLellan to the contrary notwithstanding, there is no inconsistency between acknowledging the need to fight this new terrorist phenomenon and insisting that the fight avoid needless infringements of civil liberties. Similarly, it was possible during World War II to accord the highest priority to the defeat of the Axis powers but nevertheless oppose the wholesale incarceration of all those innocent Japanese Canadians. And during the Cold War, it was possible to be committed, first and foremost, to the containment of Soviet Communism but nevertheless oppose U.S. Senator Joseph McCarthy's persecution of innocent left-wingers. It is a shame that more North Americans failed to adopt these positions. It is also a shame that Canada's 2001 minister of justice levelled such criticism at those who have been attempting to avoid the fallacies of yesteryear.

In a further response to the critics of her anti-terrorist measures, McLellan said, "I never start from the premise [that] the police set out to abuse their powers."[5] Neither, as it happens, do many critics of her legislation. As one of those critics, I, too, regard deliberate malevolence as a minority phenomenon in the Canadian police community. Indeed, I have long believed that if we ever lose our freedom in this country by erosion from within rather than invasion from without, the job will be done to us not by malevolent autocrats seeking to do bad, but by parochial bureaucrats seeking to do good.

The problem with these bureaucrats is that they become narrowly fixated on only one aspect of their role and, as a result, they neglect countervailing considerations. Thus, in the case of certain police officers, they focus essentially on achieving the desired law-enforcement results and tend to use various shortcuts to get there. Too often they overlook their accompanying obligation to intrude no further on liberty and privacy than is reasonably necessary for such purposes. McLellan's comments seem to ignore the most prevalent and recurring cause of police abuse.

By way of additionally reassuring the public that her anti-terror laws would not unduly encroach on civil liberties, McLellan asserted that "in our free and democratic society [abuse] comes to light fairly quickly."[6] Tell that to those whose mail was unlawfully opened by the Royal Canadian Mounted Police (RCMP) security service for some thirty years prior to 1972. Even at that the issue never came to light until the late 1970s.[7] And tell it to the family of social democratic leader David Lewis who, despite his profound anti-Communism, was subjected to RCMP surveillance for some fifty years because, as a committed socialist, he was "disposed to criticism of the existing political structure."[8] And even though this surveillance reportedly lasted until Lewis's death in 1981, the public did not learn of it until 2001.[9] Regrettably, the minister's assurances have been rendered hollow by such experiences.

As far as possible, therefore, it is essential that our *legislation* strike the right balance. No sophisticated democracy has any business simply trusting the authorities. In view of the nature and magnitude of the terrorist threat, it is, of course, appropriate for the law to ensure that the police have the requisite tools to do the job. It is also imperative, however, that the laws we enact don't encroach any more than is necessary on the fundamental freedoms basic to our democratic system. Accordingly, we must examine those laws themselves.

2

Expanding the Offences

THE TRIGGERING DEFINITION

The heart of Canada's special anti-terror law is its definition of "terrorist activity." Everything that follows — the prohibitions, requirements, and powers — flows from this central starting point. Unfortunately, the definition is so broad that the law can wind up targeting behaviour that does not remotely resemble what most of us think of as terrorism.

In one key part, the definition of terrorism would include certain activity that seriously disrupts "essential" services or facilities.[1] Consider, for example, the number of times that political activists — aboriginals, truckers, and farmers — have blockaded major highways in order to attract public attention to the various causes they were espousing. Without question a number of these were serious disruptions of an essential facility. Quite often such blockades were undertaken "in whole or in part for a political purpose";[2] they were designed to compel a change in government policy; and to the extent that they could have impeded fire, police, and ambulance services, they involved "a serious risk to ... health or safety."[3]

These factors appear capable of satisfying the law's definition of "terrorist activity." Of course, the defenders of the current law will be quick to point out that such disruptions would be exempt if they resulted from "advocacy, protest, dissent or stoppage of work."[4] Our lawmakers were not content, however, to draw the line at that point. Fearing that some such activism could go overboard, they made another distinction. Even "advocacy, protest, dissent or stoppage of work" will be considered "terrorist activity" if it is "intended" to produce certain "conduct or harm" such as "a serious risk to health or safety."[5] The defenders of the law will likely try to assure us that these activists would not be considered terrorists because they did not *intend* to cause such harm.

As impressive as this reply might sound at first blush, it will not suffice. According to the law, people are often presumed to intend the natural consequences of their acts.[6] Thus, in the absence of further evidence, the highway blockaders might be deemed to have *intended* to cause "a serious risk to health or safety." Although they might come up with evidence to absolve themselves, these activists could wind up experiencing an ordeal way out of proportion to their misdeeds. Even if they were ultimately cleared of "terrorist activity," it could be a veritable nightmare to have the authorities treat them as terrorists.

On the strength of a more precise interpretation, however, it might not be possible for them to be cleared of such misconduct. Even if the highway blockaders could not be said to have intended the "harm" of a serious risk to health or safety, they did intend to engage in the "conduct" — the disruption of motor traffic — that caused such harm. This outcome would flow from the fact that the governing definition talks about "conduct" *or* "harm."

On this basis, the aboriginals, truckers, and farmers in our example could well be charged — and even convicted — as terrorists. In the absence of the anti-terror law, their blockade of the highway would likely be seen as an act of "mischief," punishable by a maximum of ten years in jail. Under the anti-terror law, what they have done is subject to prosecution as "an indictable offence" committed "in association with" an organization that could now be seen as "a terrorist group." As such these activists could be jailed *for life.*[7]

In fairness I am in no way predicting that the anti-terror law will be applied against such protest activity. But I am saying that the law creates a needless risk of such an outcome, a risk our society should not incur. Nor am I advocating the immunization of such civil disobedience to legal sanction. I am simply arguing that we should not treat this misconduct as *terrorist*. Highway obstructions will remain violations of the law. There is no need to bring them within the scope of our anti-terror measures. To do so is to denigrate our sense of proportion.

Since the definition includes acts committed "in or outside Canada," there are also international implications. Towards the end of 2004, for example, there were serious upheavals in Ukraine. Some 200,000 people demonstrated in Kiev's Independence Square to protest against alleged fraud in the elections that were held there at that time.[8] Viktor Yushchenko, the candidate of the demonstrators, urged what he called "a nationwide political strike."[9] Apparently, this meant general strikes and sit-ins that had the intent of crippling the incumbent government and forcing it to concede defeat.

Is it not conceivable that such activity could cause the kind of disruption that fits squarely within the scope of *our* anti-terror law? To whatever extent, therefore, that individual Canadians provided financial and other support to the demonstrators, as many did, they might well have wound up committing a terrorist crime *in this country*. Under our definition of "terrorist activity," the democratic character of those protests could not redeem their Canadian supporters.

It appears that such excesses might be attributable, at least in part, to flaws in the then minister's thinking. During the course of the parliamentary hearings, an opposition MP asked the minister whether the definition could apply to a union that threatened to paralyze essential services with an illegal strike in order to put pressure on the government. McLellan replied partly as follows: "Your example, it's clear to me, is not intended to be caught by this definition ..."[10]

This situation seems to be one where the minister is confusing intent with effect. Since the government does not intend that the law be applied to such an example, she concludes that it won't apply. Unfortunately, history is full of situations in which police, governments, and even courts have wound up distorting, or misconstruing, the original intent of a statutory enactment. The looser the statutory language, the greater the risk of such an outcome. The misconception here is surprising in view of the minister's impressive credentials as a respected law professor.

Until this point my comments have dealt entirely with how non-violent disruptions could be caught by Canada's anti-terror law. There are also, of course, prohibitions against Canadians supporting violence in other countries. Even in this area the government's approach has been excessive.

Suppose, at long last, a democratic uprising erupted in Mainland China against the dictators who govern that country. And suppose that the uprising contained some violence. Even though such a development would likely thrill freedom-loving people around the world, and even if there was a valiant effort to avoid civilian casualties, it might well be unlawful for any Canadian to send money to the rebels.

The credit for this absurdity also belongs to Canada's anti-terror law. In the course of barring Canadians from providing various forms of assistance to ideologically motivated violence that is designed to coerce governments, this anti-terrorist prohibition omits some critical distinctions: it doesn't distinguish between pro- and anti-democratic violence. Nor at a crucial point does it differentiate between the deliberate targeting of innocent civilians and what is directed against armed combatants.

Admittedly, aid to some violent insurrections might be excused by the law's exemption for armed conflicts conducted in accordance with international law. But in the words of a 1997 amendment to the Geneva Conventions, such rebellions are apparently confined to those against "colonial domination, alien occupation, and racist regimes."[11] An indigenous uprising within China could well not qualify. The current Chinese regime is a homegrown tyranny that generally abuses its people without regard to race or ethnicity. The protesters in Tiananmen Square, for example, were subjected to an equal-opportunity massacre.

The same, of course, could be said for those dictatorships, such as the ones in North Korea and Iran, that are currently on the danger list for the Western democracies. At the moment Canadians who assisted such insurrections against those governments might also be guilty of a crime in this country. The thought boggles the mind.

Is this flaw one of the casualties of the speed with which the anti-terror bill was pushed through Parliament? This part of the definition of "terrorist activity" attracted relatively little attention. Most of the commentary dealt with the implications of the definition for various acts of non-violent civil disobedience within Canada. Comparatively little commentary was addressed to the implications of the definition for the support of Canadians regarding violence in other countries.

In this respect, consider the position of the Canadian Jewish Congress. Speaking for that group, international law scholar Ed Morgan made the following statements:

> I particularly commend the government ... for avoiding the trap of trying to define good terrorism and bad terrorism ... it should not turn on our view of international politics. The definition of terrorism, as it is in the Bill ... has clearly prohibited and criminalized *any* form of ideologically, politically, and religiously motivated violence, and in my submission that's appropriate [emphasis added].[12]

In this way, the Canadian Jewish Congress strengthened the support for the law's current definition. In view of the fact that dictatorships such as the ones in China, North Korea, and Iran may well not be removable without a certain amount of violence, why should anyone who believes in democracy be prohibited from helping with the transformation? It is hard to believe that the government of Canada or groups like the Canadian Jewish Congress directed their minds to this outcome. The most plausible explanation is that in the rush to get the bill passed there was too little time adequately to consider the implications of what they were doing.

These definitional problems precipitate the inevitable question: is the game worth the candle? How much do we really need the whole regime connected to the anti-terror law? With few exceptions, whatever we do need has been available *without* this addition to our legal system. And those few exceptions could have been adopted without all the accompanying baggage.

Why was it necessary then to engage in the semantic somersaults inherent in the definition that Canada's Parliament finally enacted? And why was it necessary to authorize such repressive crackdowns on non-violent civil disobedience at home and Canadian help to democrats abroad? In this connection, I can do no better than reproduce the recommendation officially promulgated by my organization, the Canadian Civil Liberties Association:

> To whatever extent Canadian law continues to employ the concept of terrorism, the working definition should extend no further than the following:
> (a) acts intended to cause death or serious bodily injury;
> (b) acts that deliberately target non-military personnel or those who do not direct or materially assist military personnel;
> (c) acts whose purpose is to intimidate a population or compel a government to change its behaviour; and
> (d) acts that are designed to undermine democracy, that is, the system in which government derives its authority from the freely given consent of the governed.[13]

Granted, this definition could not catch every dangerous deed that terrorists have committed, but it would nail the most serious ones. As far as any others are concerned, the conduct in question would likely be unlawful, anyway. And the police always had ample, if not excessive, power to deal with them. Thus, to whatever extent we opted for such a special regime, there would be little to lose by having the definition focus on the most deadly manifestations of the terrorist phenomenon.

The resulting definition that Parliament enacted speaks less to the genuine security needs of the country than to the obsessive proclivities of its government.

LOWERING THE THRESHOLD OF CULPABILITY

An improved definition, however, would be necessary but not sufficient. Our anti-terrorist legislation contains other provisions that would remain troubling. In this regard, it is helpful to begin by examining what the government was aiming to accomplish. Here is what then justice minister Anne McLellan said about the government's objectives:

> The insidious nature of terrorism has dictated the need for new measures. These measures must have a preventative focus, because punishing terrorist crimes after they occur is not enough. Ladies and gentlemen, the way I very simply explain this is, if we don't stop the terrorists getting on the plane, it's too late. We must be able to disable organizations before they are able to put hijackers on planes or threaten our sense of security ...[14]

Accordingly, the new legislation contains a number of new offences; they include participating in a terrorist group, facilitating terrorist activity, instructing activity that would enhance the ability of terrorist groups to carry out terrorist activities, and harbouring or concealing those who have already conducted or are likely to conduct terrorist activities. Yet even without these provisions, our criminal law has long made it an offence not only to commit the overt acts associated with terrorism, but also to attempt, conspire, counsel, aid, abet, incite, and even solicit the commission of such overt acts. It is hard, therefore, to imagine what conduct is covered by the new provisions that is not entailed by the old ones. It is also difficult to appreciate why the old enactments do not provide a sufficient ability to prevent terrorist

89

activity. Since the courts will feel some obligation to interpret the new provisions differently from the old ones, there will be an increased risk of catching non-dangerous — or at least substantially less dangerous — behaviour.

The new offence of participating in a terrorist group, for example, might wind up including in its net, behaviour such as attending dances or banquets. Moreover, the measure in question would prohibit the provision of a skill or expertise for the benefit of a terrorist group. Is this provision so broad that it could include doctors, dentists, or chiropractors? Even if a conviction might require proof of a nefarious purpose, such health providers might be rendered vulnerable to prosecution, or at least harassment, simply for doing their professional duty. This is the problem of an overly preventive focus. The further removed an offence might be from the overt conduct, the greater the risk of nailing behaviour that does not really threaten our welfare or security. Indeed, even honourable behaviour could become a casualty.

A couple of the new offences, however, do contribute something unquestionably different to the criminal law. In doing so, they might create as many problems as they purport to address. One of the new offences prohibits dealing with the property of a "terrorist group."[15] This measure could put conscientious citizens in a precarious position. Apart from those entities that appear on the government's new list of terrorist groups (more on this later), how are we to know that those with whom we plan to deal are taboo? In order to stay out of trouble, people might well avoid dealing with anyone who remotely creates suspicion. Could this result in de facto boycotts against dealing with people of Arab origin or the Muslim religion? It is not hard to imagine the injustices that could result.

Similar considerations apply to a companion provision that requires all of us to disclose to the authorities when we happen to come into possession of property owned by a terrorist entity.[16] It is one thing to impose such a duty on those, such as banks or real-estate companies, that are in the business of turning over various forms of wealth and property. It is another thing entirely to impose this way on *everybody*.

90

Again this provision puts a premium on paranoid suspicion, but it also creates even further problems. There are very few legal requirements for members of society to inform on one another. After all, freedom *of* speech is also supposed to include freedom *from* speech. There are other reasons, however, why our law generally avoids imposing such a requirement on people. Among other things, our society has long believed that a climate of compulsory informing could well erode social harmony. The more that we are required to inform, the more that people are likely to be suspicious of one another.

There is little indication that this measure was adequately scrutinized when Parliament was considering the legislation. Did anyone seriously ask whether such a measure was necessary? Without it the law still bars contributing to, raising money for and, in many other ways, serving the interests of terrorist groups. Moreover, in the post-9/11 climate, we could expect a sizable increase in *voluntary* reporting.

As far as the creation of new offences is concerned, therefore, the new law either adds virtually nothing to the old law or it threatens needlessly to erode our freedoms.

3

Expanding the Powers

THE OSTRACIZING OF TERROR SUSPECTS

Another method the government has devised for preventing the damage that terrorists can cause involves the creation of new powers. In this connection, former justice minister Anne McLellan said that "a first step in disabling and dismantling terrorist groups is to identify them. [The anti-terror bill] … sets up a distinct procedure to enable the [government] to create by regulation a list of entities" involved in "terrorist activities."[1] The list is to be published so that everyone may know who is on it. As indicated, it immediately becomes an offence for everyone else to have certain dealings with those on the list.

In every case, the decision to list is made by the government on the recommendation of the solicitor general (now the minister of public safety and emergency preparedness).[2] No hearing is required and, therefore, no evidence need then be produced. While the targets may subsequently challenge the listing in court, a lot of damage could be suffered before that happened. One of the most contentious features of this provision is that individuals, as well as organizations, could wind up on the list. While organizations have limited functions to perform, individuals have ordinary lives to lead.

In this connection, consider what happened to Liban Hussein, a Canadian citizen from Somalia. He had lived in Canada for several years, during which time he built up a business that managed to support himself, his wife, his children, and a number of other relatives. One day he suddenly found himself on the list. As soon as that happened, his assets were frozen, he was jailed, and the United States began extradition proceedings against him.[3] And, of course, it also became a crime to have certain dealings with him. A few months later he was just as suddenly cleared of all wrongdoing. The government declared that there was no evidence whatsoever linking this man to terrorism. But, according to his lawyer, he had lost his business and his life lay in ruins.[4]

In view of the law's capacity to devastate people this way, it is hard to be consoled by McLellan's assurance that "being on the list does not itself constitute a criminal offence."[5] But being on the list can effectively transform a person into a virtual pariah. And that can happen without ever convicting the person of any unlawful conduct.

Despite what such a measure can do — and has done — to people, the most serious controversies it has produced since its enactment concern *exclusions* from the list. Instead of complaining that the government has acquired the power unilaterally to destroy those it puts on the list, critics have rebuked the government for its failure to include certain entities. There was quite a controversy, for example, over the length of time it took to list the suspected terror organizations, Hezbollah and the Tamil Tigers.[6]

The most serious criticism that the *National Post* could make of this power concerned the fact that it "leaves in the hands of cabinet, not police agencies or administrative officials, the determination of what groups are and are not terrorist in nature."[7] If this newspaper had its way, therefore, the police agency responsible for imposing fifty years of surveillance on David Lewis would acquire the power unilaterally to ostracize people. One can only feel gratitude that some editorial writers never get into government.

Testifying before the parliamentary committee considering the anti-terror bill, then solicitor general Lawrence McAulay made a separate attempt to console MPs about this power. He pointed out that there is "a review mechanism to ensure the integrity of the list process."[8] Then came the punch line: "*I* must review this list every two years ... [emphasis added]"[9] I can imagine how breathlessly the MPs were hanging on to the solicitor general's every word. Among other things, we must be impressed with McAulay's sense of drama.

Then, almost as an anti-climax, McAulay announced that the legislation would have another safeguard: "the list must be subject to federal court review ..."[10] This remark looks as though it was composed by a particularly skillful bureaucrat. While the existence of federal court review would likely mollify many people, it should be noted that such review would not necessarily occur in every case. Note that the solicitor general said the process was *subject to* such review. That doesn't mean the review *would* occur; it simply means it *could* occur. A review would require, however, that the aggrieved person take the initiative. The problem is that, once a listing has done its damage, the targets may no longer have the resources or the stamina to sustain a court fight.

In a conversation with an Ottawa mandarin during the fall of 2001, I particularly questioned the power to list individuals, apart from organizations. The reply questioned whether I would have any particular objection to the listing of individuals such as Osama bin Laden. I confess that the prospect of listing the likes of bin Laden could hardly get my knickers in a twist, then or now. But why, I have continued to ask, should the government be able to exercise such power over individual citizens and permanent residents?

Moreover, how necessary is this power to the fight against terrorism? After all, those slated for the list are likely to be under intense surveillance already. This would likely increase the ability of police and security forces to anticipate and, therefore, to intercept the targets' harmful behaviour. And, as for crippling the financial capacity of suspected terrorists, why would it not suffice to provide for the freezing of their assets after *a court* has ruled on the reasonableness of such an encroachment? I am not aware that the parliamentary debates on the anti-terror bill ever raised such issues with any of the ministers.

PREVENTIVE DETENTION

While the listing power attracted relatively little attention during the parliamentary debates, the preventive detention power attracted a lot. In some respects, this reaction may seem peculiar because, in all, those suspected of involvement in terrorism can only be held for seventy-two hours before a bail hearing is convened. Even at that they must be brought before a judge within the first twenty-four hours or as soon as possible thereafter.[11]

By comparison, consider the fact that, at the time of the 1970 FLQ crisis in Quebec, the initial period of preventive detention was twenty-one days and it was then modified to seven days.[12] The critical difference, however, is that the rules established at that time were acknowledged to be emergency ones and they were explicitly temporary. They were made subject to expiry within a few months. By contrast, our current anti-terrorist legislation has no such deadline. The preventive detention power is slated for review, not expiry, after five years, not a few months.[13]

The current power contains another feature that seems rather curious: as a condition of securing their release, those arrested may be required to sign a bond that they will observe certain conditions designed to preserve the peace.[14] In view of the fact that the Criminal Code already provided for such peace bonds in anticipation of sexual assaults, personal injury offences, or "criminal organization" offences,[15] Professor Martin Friedland might have been right when he suggested that "it is not a great stretch to carry the technique over to fear of a terrorist offence."[16] On the other hand, it is hard to take this measure seriously. Imagine the suicide terrorists of 9/11 feeling obliged to observe the restraints of a peace bond they signed! Similarly, imagine those terrorists having any qualms about signing a bond they had no intention of observing!

REQUIRING INVESTIGATIVE ASSISTANCE

Our anti-terrorist legislation also requires that people answer investigative questions put to them by the police if there are "reasonable grounds" to believe such people have information about a terrorist crime that has been, or will be, committed.[17] There are safeguards: the proceedings are presided over by a judge, the compulsory testimony may generally not be tendered against the person who provides it, and such person is entitled to the assistance of a lawyer.[18]

It is one thing to compel testimony at an adjudicative hearing such as a criminal trial where the issues are reasonably well circumscribed. It is another thing entirely to do so at an investigative hearing where the issues are largely still to be determined. In the latter situation, the probe would be much less focused. Thus, we could expect much greater intrusions into the lives of those compelled to speak. For these purposes, their own innocence wouldn't matter. Suppose, for example, that Tom, who is not a suspect, is reasonably believed to know the whereabouts or activities of Dick or Harry, who are suspects. In such circumstances, Tom, despite his own innocence, could well be forced to testify about Dick and/or Harry. In the process, he could wind up revealing many personal details of his own life.

The prospect of such a scenario is one reason why our criminal law tradition has generally opposed any obligation to speak for investigative purposes. Our system has tried over the years to prevent government fishing expeditions into the lives of innocent people. Since the police have long managed without the power at issue here, the need for it appears questionable.

During the fall of 2001, the Canadian Civil Liberties Association proposed a compromise: such evidence might be compelled not to resolve misdeeds already committed, but to prevent perils imminently expected.[19] The government was not interested in such compromises; the new power was adopted intact.

ELECTRONIC BUGGING

Parliament has also expanded the power to employ electronic surveillance. Judicial warrants are now available to authorize wiretaps and electronic bugs for some of the new offences related to terrorism.[20] There are serious questions as to why this power has been considered necessary. Without it the Canadian Security Intelligence Service (CSIS) is able to get such warrants to use electronic bugging for what the CSIS Act calls "activities ... in support ... of acts of serious violence ... for the purpose of achieving a political, religious, or ideological objective within Canada or a foreign state."[21] It is obvious that this terminology is wide enough to include suspected terrorism. Indeed, since it includes *all* violence with such objectives, it reaches well beyond terrorism; it could potentially even be used against those who are *fighting* terrorism.

What then has changed? Until the advent of the 2001 anti-terror law, only CSIS was eligible to use electronic bugging against the breadth of activities described above. Now, however, the *police* have also acquired such bugging power. Why does that make a difference? When CSIS uses this power, it is subject to auditing by the independent Security Intelligence Review Committee (SIRC).[22] But no such audit function is currently applicable to the greatest number of Canada's police forces. Intended or not, this new bugging power permits an end run around the monitoring activities of SIRC. Accordingly, I have no difficulty concluding that Canada would have been better off without such additional power.

The anti-terrorist statute also provides that the duration of bugging periods for terrorist offences will be one year instead of — as it is for many other matters — sixty days.[23] That means, if the police wish to renew their authority to wiretap, they have a year instead of just sixty days to seek a judge's permission. Martin Friedland noted that such changes "are already in the Criminal Code for offences involving criminal organizations." In his view, "if they are warranted for such offences, they are even more acceptable for terrorism offences ..."[24]

I agree with Friedland. In my view, however, the expanded period is not justified in *either* situation. Where was the need? When is the last time a judge refused to grant such authority to the police? It would be impossible to fill a thimble with the number of times this has happened in the more than thirty years that our law has involved judges in wiretap decisions. I think it is fair to say, therefore, that the *only* contribution made by this provision is to reduce judicial supervision of one of the most privacy-intrusive instruments in the police arsenal.

THE SECRECY OF PROCEEDINGS

Among the new powers created by the post-9/11 anti-terror law is one that can impose a veil of secrecy over information that would otherwise be available in a variety of proceedings. As soon as parties, witnesses, or certain officials can reasonably anticipate the prospect that information bearing upon certain national interests may be tendered at a hearing, there is an obligation to notify the attorney general of Canada. Once so notified, the attorney general can take steps to keep the information from ever emerging into public view.[25] Indeed, the power appears to be so broad that it might even prevent the existence of the proceeding itself from becoming a matter of public knowledge.

This power has the capacity to damage some of our most precious freedoms. Consider the right to a fair hearing. Among other things, such a right must mean a reasonable opportunity for impugned persons to defend themselves. A competent and adequate defence requires access to all relevant evidence and information. Knowledge of such information enables those who are impugned to explain, rebut, justify, maximize, and minimize. The less access there is to relevant information, the less able impugned people are to defend themselves — indeed, the more helpless they become in the face of enormous state strength.

Another way in which this new power undermines the right to a fair hearing is by keeping the *public* in the dark. When abuses in the process are transmitted to the public, pressures for rectification are more readily created. In fact, the knowledge that the public is watching often acts as a deterrent against the propensity to abuse in the first place. Not surprisingly, therefore, jurists have declared that publicity is the "soul" of justice.

Even apart from the fairness of hearings, the power at issue here can undermine the viability of our democracy. After all, public scrutiny is the prerequisite of accountability. To whatever extent critical information is kept from the public, the wielders of power can misbehave with impunity. Secrecy is the compatriot of tyranny.

Supporters of this scheme would undoubtedly point to the provision whereby a judge of the Federal Court of Appeal can overrule the attorney general about such exclusions of evidence.[26] But the grounds for the exclusions are very broad. They include material "in relation to a foreign entity ... national defence, or national security."[27] This could exclude information that touches only trivially upon such legitimate government interests. A defence document, for example, might be withheld even if it is essential for the fairness of a particular case or scrutiny of a government deed and even though the document contains *nothing* damaging to our defence interests. Moreover, material that is simply "in relation to a foreign entity" conceivably could keep out information on the basis of nothing more than idle gossip about a country other than Canada.

Earlier on there is a power by which a Federal Court trial judge can keep information out of view if its disclosure would be "injurious" to international relations, national defence, or national security.[28] Why should mere injury, no matter how inconsequential, suffice to overcome the pivotal rights involved? Even serious injury, however, might not always constitute a sufficient criterion. Consider the case of serious injury to international relations. The problem here is that "international relations" is so broad that it could include even sports events, arts festivals, and commercial interactions. These are conceivably important activities, to be sure, but not all of them could be important enough to deny due process for impugned parties and information for the public.

While the court in a criminal case is entitled to effectively acquit an accused person if it considers the excluded information vital to a fair trial, no such remedy is available for any other proceeding.[29] Criminal trials are not the only processes that can wind up perpetrating substantial encroachments on people. So, too, for example, can deportations. Indeed, sometimes this process can effectively send people to torture and death in other countries. No matter what damage the permissible exclusion of information could cause to the fairness of a deportation hearing, however, the adjudicator is unable to rescue the impugned person.

Only the most vital interests of our society could possibly justify the consequent damage to the freedoms involved. For such purposes, it might arguably be acceptable to exclude information if its disclosure could be expected to cause "serious injury to the physical safety and defence of the country." Unfortunately, though, the law now permits far less important values to override these basic freedoms.

One of the most damning criticisms of this power to conceal information emerged in a judgment from the Federal Court. In commenting on a case before him, the chief justice of that court made the following observations: "Under the current law, no one is to disclose that a notice of application ... has been filed with the Federal Court.... Put simply, not even the Court can acknowledge publicly that it is seized of [such a] proceeding. This can lead to unintended, even absurd, consequences."[30]

THE SECURITY OF INFORMATION

In late January 2004, ten RCMP officers reportedly ransacked the home of *Ottawa Citizen* reporter Juliet O'Neill.[31] For five hours they searched her house, went through her personal belongings, downloaded her computer's hard drive, and removed files, spiral notebooks, address books, and phone books. According to the press, the officers were trying to find the source of an alleged leak of information stemming from an earlier story that O'Neill had written. The story dealt with Maher Arar, a Canadian citizen who had been deported to his native Syria by U.S. authorities after being intercepted in New York.[32] It has also been revealed that Arar was incarcerated and tortured during his stay in Syria.[33]

Although O'Neill has not been charged with any offence as of the date of this writing, her editor and lawyers have expressed the fear that she could face such a charge under the Security of Information Act that was passed in the wake of 9/11.[34] That statute, a successor to the notorious Official Secrets Act, contains broad prohibitions against the disclosure and unauthorized possession of government materials. Moreover, it carries a maximum penalty of fourteen years in prison.[35] The search warrant, which authorized the police search of O'Neill's premises, was based entirely on this controversial law.

The Security of Information Act prohibits the disclosure of "secret ... information ... that has been ... obtained in contravention of this Act ..."[36] It is suspected that an employee of the RCMP had unlawfully leaked the information in question to O'Neill.[37] The act of leaking could be viewed as a violation of this statute. And so, therefore, could the subsequent disclosures contained in O'Neill's story. This could also make her guilty of receiving the information "in contravention of this Act."[38] Incredibly, the mere, passive act of receiving such information could implicate her unless she could prove that the communication to her "was contrary to [her] desire."

The scope of this law is nothing short of draconian. The word *secret* is nowhere defined. Thus, anyone who discloses information emanating from the bowels of government has to contend with the risk of a fourteen-year jail sentence.

Yet our collective experience tells us that it is very important for the public to enjoy a timely right of access to much, if not most, of what is going on inside of government. A well-timed news story has the capacity to exert just the kind of pressure needed to correct misconduct and redress injustice in high places. If legislation of this kind had existed in the United States at the time of the Watergate scandals, Richard Nixon might never have been driven from the American presidency. After all, the disclosures of government wrongdoing published in the *Washington Post* newspaper contributed substantially to Nixon's historic resignation. Even if civil servants who leak information to the press might legitimately be subject to employment discipline, that doesn't mean the press should be *criminally* liable for subsequently publishing such material.

Nor is it necessary to remove *all* such impediments on the flow of government information in order to oppose the *breadth* of this one. Unfortunately, however, there is no provision expressly limiting the prohibitions against press disclosures to the most sensitive of state secrets.

Moreover, the law does not include any requirement for the documents in question to contain any markings indicating that they are intended to be "secret" or "classified."

How then is anyone to know that it is forbidden to reveal their contents? The safe response is simply to desist from publishing such government material. Not a very helpful course of action for a democracy to adopt. But even if there were some markings on a document, there is also no systematic way to question the validity of the designation. The result is that the press can be unwarrantedly muzzled in what it can write and the public can be unjustifiably deprived of what it can learn.

And why in the world should the passive receipt of information *by itself* be a crime? It is one thing to penalize people for counselling, conspiring, inciting, and attempting to obtain what they know they should not have. But it is another thing entirely to penalize them for mere receipt. Nor is it any answer to provide accused people with the escape hatch of proving that their possession was "contrary to [their] desire." Guilty desire hardly warrants the awesome risk of imprisonment. Many newspaper reporters, indeed many curious citizens, might well desire to know government secrets. But without some transition from desire to action, it is unconscionable that people can suffer the imposition of criminal sanctions and the possibility of a fourteen-year jail sentence.

In the late 1970s, the Official Secrets Act provoked considerable controversy. It was roundly attacked from the Right, the Left, and the Centre as a needless threat to some of our most fundamental freedoms. It was expected, therefore, that this law would be repealed or at least substantially amended. Inexplicably, that never happened. Instead, in the wake of 9/11, its worst features were re-enacted.

CONTROLLING ACCESS TO INTERNATIONAL CONFERENCES

Within a two- or three-year period at the beginning of the new millennium, Canada played host to at least three international conferences involving high-level diplomats and even heads of state. Coupled with the events of 9/11, the prospect of Canada replaying this role produced another piece of legislation in 2002 — a provision dealing with the security of intergovernmental conferences.[39] To provide such security, the RCMP "may take appropriate measures, including controlling, limiting, or prohibiting access to any area to the extent and in a manner that is reasonable in the circumstances."[40]

This creates quite a mandate. Nowhere does this new law provide the slightest guidance as to how to interpret such terminology. And nowhere is there even an attempt to spell out the various interests that need to be accommodated. Effectively, all this measure says is that the RCMP may do what is "reasonable." Remarkably, the government insists that "this legislation does not confer 'new' authority on the RCMP.... Rather ... it clarifies" the existing authority.[41]

Some clarification. For an illuminating example of the kind of clarity produced by words like this, consider an incident at the Hughes Inquiry into the RCMP's handling of the protests at the 1997 APEC Conference in Vancouver. Under questioning an RCMP inspector who had been involved in the removal of lawfully displayed protest signs testified that he was influenced not by the Charter of Rights and Freedoms, but by what was "reasonable under the circumstances."[42] Thus, this officer justified his infringement of constitutional freedoms on the basis of the very criteria that appear in this new law — criteria the government sees as a clarification of the old law.

In any event, why should the law, old or new, repose so much power in the RCMP? After all, the decision to keep people out of publicly accessible areas involves more than security considerations. It also involves a wide variety of other interests: those of homeowners, businesses, workers, tourists, and yes, protesters. Except for emergency and frontline situations, there is something questionable about putting the police in the position of adjudicating among all of these competing interests.

The usual role of the police in a democracy is to enforce the judgments made by others, not to make such judgments themselves. The risk created by this law is that the RCMP's decisions would be — or at least appear to be — designed primarily to ease the burdens of the RCMP's job. As sympathetic as any of us may be, we must recognize that these interests must be balanced against others.

Consider the legitimate interests of protesters who wish to demonstrate. (For these purposes, only *lawful* protest is worthy of consideration.) In order to be effective, the protesters will often seek to create an atmosphere of political tension and censure on those whose policies they are trying to influence. This could entail getting as close as they can to the action. Of course, they cannot be allowed to come so close that they can physically intimidate, but they must be close enough to politically castigate. That means the protesters must be at least periodically seen and heard if not, at any time, felt or smelt.

But the interest of the police will be to get the protesters as far away as possible. Obviously, it is much easier to provide security and control traffic when the protesters are far away rather than close at hand. But as a labour activist once remarked, it is improper in a democracy for any of us to be the umpires of our own ballgame. That is why, apart from emergency and frontline situations, the police should not be establishing these conference perimeters.

In the first instance, this role should be exercised by someone who has *political* responsibility. Ideally, a cabinet minister should have to carry the can for adjudicating among the competing interests affected. But because even the interpretations made by cabinet ministers would look as though they were influenced more by what is popular than by what is right, ultimate approval should be required by the courts. Of course, the interpretation of applicable statutes and the adjudication of competing interests are exactly what judges do all the time. Since these intergovernmental conferences are often planned months, if not years, in advance, there will usually be sufficient time for plans to be created, notice to be provided, and hearings to be conducted.

Considering the centrality of the right of effective protest — not to mention the other interests that could be involved — such procedures should become mandatory to establish these conference perimeters. By allowing the police this kind of power, the government denigrates the importance of our fundamental freedoms. Such power also puts the police in an unwarrantedly contentious position.

In response to such criticisms, the government contended that "traditionally, prior judicial authorizations have been required ... only when the police wish to use particularly invasive tools such as entry and search [and] wiretapping ..."[43] This reply is unimpressive. Among other things, the government appears to have overlooked generations of experience with injunctions. These are court orders that have been used in labour and other protest situations to regulate picket lines and demonstrations so as to adjust the equities between the competing parties and to protect the general welfare. Even apart from this precedent, the government should be aiming to avoid a situation where affected parties, such as the police, are empowered to adjudicate disputes involving their own interests. I would have thought that such an objective was elementary to the rule of law.

By way of further defending its decision to keep this power within the RCMP, the government made the following statement:

"In light of the necessity for the police to make "on-the-spot" decisions to protect ... the functioning of an international event, it would be both impractical and improper to require the police to obtain judicial or ministerial approval before being able to respond with an appropriate security measure."[44]

However, the need for the police to make on-the-spot decisions is not a rarity even where injunctions, search warrants, and wiretap authorizations are concerned. There is no incompatibility. The prior authorization sets out a general framework within which it is always understood that the police might have to make emergency or frontline decisions. Why then couldn't the issues here be handled in a similar manner? In order to avoid what is obviously fair, the government has resorted to conspicuously lame rationalizations.

MORE ANTI-HATE MEASURES

The government's anti-terrorist legislation contains a feature that could well appeal to certain groups with rather disparate interests: on the one hand, Jews and Israelis; on the other hand, Arabs and Muslims. Pointing out that "discrimination against persons of any religious or racial or ethnic background will not be tolerated," then justice minister Anne McLellan told her fellow parliamentarians that the anti-terror bill provides for the deletion of hate material "from computer systems such as an Internet site."[45] This provision could well have been designed to address some of the anxiety that Arabs and Muslims were experiencing in the aftermath of 9/11. It certainly accorded with a long-standing proposal by the Canadian Jewish Congress.

Too bad. Despite this measure's apparent popularity with both of these minority constituencies, the government should not have adopted it. Instead of moving to increase Canada's anti-hate measures, the government should have started to reduce them.

The problem with these provisions is their ability to threaten legitimate freedom of speech. Even though this freedom is not an absolute, it nevertheless engages the guts of the democratic system. It enables any of us to appeal for public support in our efforts to redress our grievances. As indicated earlier, freedom of speech is based on the experience that injustice is less likely to endure, or even to emerge, in an atmosphere of open public debate.

The special problem with the anti-hate law is the unavoidable vagueness of the word *hatred*. It would have been more acceptable for the law to address incitements to *violence*. But *hatred* can create a legal morass. We know that freedom of speech is often most important when it expresses strong disapproval. But where does strong disapproval end and *hatred* begin? The risk, therefore, is that this law could wind up targeting expression that doesn't bear the slightest resemblance to the invective of hate mongers. Indeed, this has already happened. Among those harassed by Canada's thirty-year-old anti-hate law are anti-American protesters, French Canadian nationalists, anti-apartheid activists, a pro-Zionist book, and a Jewish community leader.[46]

Significantly, some of the formulations in the anti-terror bill did not satisfy the Canadian Jewish Congress. It complained that one of the powers was too narrow; it would be "limited to hatred." "Rather," the congress argued, the "power should include 'both hatred *and* contempt' [emphasis added]."[47] For the Canadian Jewish Congress, therefore, the idea is to expand the power to encroach on free speech. Indeed, the power proposed by the congress would delete from the Internet and certain other places, material "that is likely to expose … persons to hatred or contempt" on grounds such as race, religion, and ethnicity.[48]

If enacted, such measures might well not require a "wilful" intent as the general anti-hate law does. Similarly, they might not provide a defence for truth or reasonable belief in the truth of the statements at issue. On this basis, truthful discussions of racial, religious, and ethnic warfare in Bosnia, Rwanda, or Northern Ireland could very well run afoul of such an enactment. Couldn't some such discussions be seen as "likely to expose" Serbs, Croats, Muslims, Hutus, Tutsis, Catholics, or Protestants to "hatred or contempt"?

Ironically, this very power sought by the Canadian Jewish Congress might be capable of damaging even the interests of the Jewish people. Within the past number of years (both before and after 9/11), reputable scholars and writers have increasingly related how government publications in Arab countries such as Egypt and Saudi Arabia are carrying material of an extremely anti-Semitic character.[49] Would not any information that told us about such anti-Semitic literature be "likely to expose" Egyptians and Saudi Arabians to "hatred or contempt"? Under the measure proposed by this Jewish organization, such information could arguably be subject to forcible removal from the Internet — an outcome obviously incompatible with Jewish interests.

Consider also some of the articles published in the American Jewish conservative magazine *Commentary*. The Jewish writer Daniel Pipes, for example, has warned about the threats to American democracy from mainstream elements in the Muslim communities of the United States.[50] The following is illustrative of what Pipes has said on the subject: "what is not open to question is that, whatever the majority of Muslim Americans may believe, most of the *organized* Muslim community agrees with … building an Islamic state in America. To put it another way, the major Muslim organizations in this country are in the hands of extremists."[51]

Couldn't such statements be considered "likely to expose" Muslims on this continent at least to "contempt"? Significantly, just prior to making a speech at Toronto's York University, Daniel Pipes was advised by a police detective about the risk of infringing the even less broad anti-hate provision of the Criminal Code.[52] The writings of Daniel Pipes in this regard are not unlike some of the articles that have been penned by *National Post* columnist Robert Fulford.[53] It isn't necessary to agree with Pipes and Fulford in order to acknowledge that they are eminent writers whose messages, right or wrong, no legitimate democracy has any business suppressing.

PERMISSIBLE LAW-BREAKING

Despite all these excesses in Canada's anti-terror legislation, the *National Post* editorialized in the other direction. Speaking of the legislation, the *Post* said "our greatest concern ... is not that it will go too far, but that it will not go far enough." In this regard, the editorial particularly complained that "undercover agents are hampered by the fact they are not generally permitted to break the law in the service of apprehending a criminal or infiltrating a conspiracy." Indeed, the *Post* complained that "[the anti-terror bill] does not deal with undercover agents at all."[54]

True, it doesn't. But Bill C-24 does.

This bill was introduced in a session of Parliament several months *before* 9/11 and subsequently became law.[55] Although Bill C-24 was created to deal with criminal organizations, particularly of the biker variety, its provisions are wide enough to cover terrorist organizations. And its powers are enormous. Certain police officers are given wide latitude to break the law. To do this, all they need is "reasonable grounds" to believe the offence they are planning to commit is "reasonable and proportional" to the offence they are seeking to resolve.[56] For these purposes they won't even need a warrant from a judge.[57]

The power is so wide that it could victimize totally innocent people. Yes, there are limits. The police will not be allowed, for example, to commit crimes causing death or bodily harm.[58] In certain circumstances, however, Bill C-24 *explicitly* authorizes the commission of offences resulting in "loss of or serious damage to property." This could happen even if the property owner was completely innocent.[59]

In the 1970s, Canadians were scandalized to learn that, in order to carry out one of their intelligence investigations, the RCMP in Quebec had burned down a barn belonging to a private citizen. They did this to force those under surveillance to arrange a planned meeting in a place that was more susceptible to electronic bugging than was the barn. At the time the Mounties were rebuked for resorting to such tactics, but under

Bill C-24 they might legally become arsonists once again.[60] And so might all other police.

These comments are not designed to oppose any and all police law-breaking no matter what might be involved. Indeed, in some situations the law already permits a certain amount of it. Canada's narcotics legislation was recently amended, for example, so that the police may now assume the role of traffickers during undercover drug investigations.[61] But there is a world of difference between a limited power to break the law in certain carefully circumscribed situations and the kind of general power contained in Bill C-24.

Even in the war against terrorism such open-ended power is unconscionable. To be authorized, police law-breaking should, at the very least, be seen as *necessary*, not simply as "reasonable and proportional." Apart from what the law has always permitted, acts and threats of physical violence should be explicitly forbidden. Nor should the police be allowed to instigate even non-violent illegalities. It is one thing during an undercover operation to "play along" with a fraud or a theft, but it is another thing entirely for a police officer to *initiate* such misconduct.

Police officers should also be barred from committing unlawful acts against innocent victims without a particularly strong basis to believe that, if the victims knew, they would consent. Consider, for example, those police infiltrators in a racist organization who participated in the painting of swastikas on the homes of certain black and Jewish people.[62] If those homeowners had known, would they have approved of such police action in order to apprehend their racist tormenters? But no such safeguards have found their way into this legislation. It is hard to believe that moderate Canada adopted so much law-breaking power to fight not terrorists, but biker gangs.

4

The Adequacy of the Safeguards

THE FATE OF THE "SUNSET" PROPOSAL

Upon introducing amendments to the government's major anti-terror bill, then justice minister Anne McLellan made the following statement: "it has been important to debate this Bill thoroughly because it does deal with fundamental issues of human security and rights and freedoms. To pass this Bill in the absence of an extensive debate would have been inappropriate and careless."[1]

Who was she kidding? As noted earlier, the bill contained more than 150 pages of complex measures. McLellan made the above statement on November 20, 2001. The bill had been first introduced in mid-October of that same year. There simply hadn't been time for an "extensive debate."

Yes, there had been two rounds of parliamentary committee hearings in both the House of Commons and the Senate. But that sounds more impressive than it was. Those who were testifying on the bill were usually confined to some ten to fifteen minutes for their opening presentations. And although the hearings might have lasted an hour and a half, the time had to be shared with anywhere from two to four other presenters. After the initial presentations, discussion took the form of questions and answers. Since the MPs and senators were asking the questions, they usually determined what issues would be addressed. The result was that certain matters were repetitively discussed, while other matters were hardly touched. In view of the size of the bill and the complexity of the measures it contained, there was too little opportunity to debate the implications of the new law, never mind to digest them.

These considerations gave rise to the recommendation that the bill include a "sunset" clause. Under such a clause, all of the new measures would automatically expire within a certain period unless, by then, they had been re-enacted. On the one hand, this clause would immediately give the government the power it sought to deal with terrorism; on the other hand, it would pressure the government to reintroduce, in more manageable segments, those measures it sought to retain, so that at long last there would be a more meaningful parliamentary and public debate.

The response to this proposal overflowed with fallacies. According to the Canadian Police Association, such a clause should be resisted because terrorism is with us for keeps and "will not be extinguished."[2] This objection is a striking example of what logicians call a non sequitur. How does it follow that, even if terrorism should linger on in perpetuity, these specific anti-terrorist measures will also be needed forever? Indeed, there is no necessary contradiction between attributing indefinite longevity to terrorism and repealing *all* of these special anti-terrorist measures. The issue is always the extent to which various measures are needed in the anti-terrorist fight.

A second reason advanced by the Canadian Police Association against adopting a sunset clause concerns the length of time that may be involved to investigate and prosecute various terrorist activities. According to this argument, the possible repeal of any such anti-terrorist measure "would deter the initiation of investigations in the latter stages of that period and render the law increasingly useless."[3] But it would not require the genius of a legal Einstein to provide for such contingencies in any sunset clause that would be proposed.

Echoing the police association, then justice minister McLellan added that the war against terrorism "is a continuous ... one,"[4] as though that meant each measure against it also had

114

to be continuous. McLellan also argued that since the new anti-terror measures "comply with the Canadian Charter of Rights and Freedoms ... a sunset clause is not necessary to ensure their compliance."[5] There are competent constitutional lawyers in this country who have expressed somewhat less certainty that every single new anti-terrorist measure would survive a Charter challenge.[6] But even if they could, McLellan needs to be reminded that the Charter represents the minimum of what is acceptable for civil-liberties purposes. As I have attempted to indicate above, there are many undesirable features in the new anti-terror law, and there are real doubts about the need for all of them.

In the result, the government agreed to impose a sunset clause on only two of the anti-terrorist measures: the ones dealing with expanded preventive detention and the obligation to testify at investigative hearings.[7] Untouched by this process are the power to publicly list people as terrorist supporters, the prohibition against dealing with such people, and the obligation to inform, among others. Moreover, instead of becoming operative after one year as many of the critics had proposed, this sunset clause would take effect after five years.

Even at that the re-enactment would be handled not by the usual parliamentary process, but by a simple resolution adopted by a majority of each chamber. McLellan's decision to bypass the usual process reflected her "concern that the expiry could otherwise occur in urgent circumstances where it is clear that the provisions should continue."[8] It is hard to figure out what she was so worried about. Even if the country faced a dire emergency, the government could always invoke the emergency measures law and thereby clothe itself with the powers it thought were necessary. The uptight mentality evinced by the government here reminds me of a comment once made by a friend of mine: it isn't enough for these government people to wear a belt and then put on suspenders; they also have to walk around holding their pants up.

MECHANISMS OF OVERSIGHT

Critics of the government's anti-terror measures also urged additional oversight mechanisms to ensure that enforcement did not go overboard. This recommendation got nowhere. Both the justice minister and the Canadian Association of Chiefs of Police argued that there is *already* adequate oversight of police conduct. According to the chiefs, "further provisions would be duplicitous, [*sic*] rather than productive."[9] Remarkably, the chiefs went on to cite, as an example of the adequacy of current accountability mechanisms, the situation in Ontario. Yet it was in this very province some four years earlier that the relatively independent civilian complaints system was legislatively abolished.[10]

Admittedly, there are, as the chiefs argued, police services boards "made up of members of the public appointed by the provincial government and the municipal elected representatives."[11] While such a mechanism might well be necessary, it is hardly sufficient. As an agency that must constantly live with the police, one of its major propensities will be to avoid confrontation with them. After all, the avoidance of unpleasantness is an ongoing aspect of human nature. This tendency is often compounded when the police are involved. Conflict with police entails a significant risk at least of social disapproval. As public protectors, the police enjoy considerable popularity. Thus, their civilian masters not infrequently shrink into the woodwork when asked to assert their authority.

The chiefs also cited the criminal courts that, in their view, would dismiss the relevant charges "and directly sanction police misconduct."[12] This contention is somewhat of an exaggeration. Police misconduct rarely precipitates the direct acquittal of those who are being prosecuted. It does periodically produce the exclusion of evidence from certain criminal trials, and that could produce an acquittal. But evidence acquired through police misconduct will not *always* be excluded and such exclusions do not invariably lead to acquittals.

Moreover, the criminal courts do not have the capacity to investigate. So many of the conflicts between civilians and the police involve conflicts of evidence. Getting to the truth of such disputes often requires good old-fashioned investigations — an exercise courts are not structured to perform. In any event, not all, or even most, issues of possible police abuse will come to the criminal courts. The perpetrators of such abuse are not routinely prosecuted. Indeed, in our current anti-terror era where preventive law enforcement is the preferred option, the *goal* is to avoid prosecution.

Another mechanism of accountability mentioned by the chiefs association is civil litigation. Again necessary but not sufficient. It is true that a whopping damage award could go a long way to tame excesses of police behaviour. But civil law suits can be daunting and expensive. And again the capacity to investigate is not there. That crucial ingredient generally has to be supplied through the resources of the aggrieved civilians themselves. Few of them will have such resources.

The Canadian Association of Chiefs of Police referred also to our various human-rights commissions at both federal and provincial levels. They, of course, can provide publicly subsidized investigations. But their narrow jurisdiction makes them inadequate for oversight purposes. In addition to establishing who did what to whom, human-rights commissions must also prove that the impugned deeds were committed for reasons of discrimination on the basis, for example, of race, creed, ethnicity, gender, and so on. That, of course, is no easy task.

Undoubtedly, an exacerbating factor here is the backlog of cases that have accumulated in the files of these government agencies. Considering the rate at which the human-rights commissions are able to process their complaints, it could take years to produce a result. By then, of course, the key parties could well have departed from this planet. Thus, vindication might have to be enjoyed by the complainants' executors.

Although the chiefs failed to mention it, Ontario has the Special Investigations Unit (SIU), a non-police agency that conducts initial investigations. But its mandate is criminal, not disciplinary. Since juries have evinced a considerable reluctance to convict police officers in such situations, discipline would likely be the more hopeful route.

In this regard, the chiefs cited the Ontario Civilian Commission on Police Services (OCCOPS). According to the chiefs, OCCOPS "is a civilian-appointed, quasi-judicial tribunal which oversees police discipline and public complaints."[13] But even if the performance of OCCOPS inspired the requisite public confidence, the complaints system in Ontario has been notoriously "cop-heavy."

Consider how the Ontario complaints system works.[14] When a complaint first arrives, who assesses it to determine whether it is worthy of handling or should be dismissed as frivolous, vexatious, or out of time? The chief or the chief's designate. If the complaint is considered worthy of handling, who investigates it? The police. After the investigation, who assesses the results to determine what to do next, that is, to dismiss the complaint as "unsubstantiated," to attempt an informal resolution, or to order a hearing into the merits? The chief or the chief's designate. If the complaint is considered worthy of a hearing, who presides? The chief or the chief's designate. If there is a hearing, who prosecutes? The police. And who adjudicates? The chief or the chief's designate.

The only time the aggrieved civilian can have a live hearing before someone other than the police is after the adjudication by the chief or the chief's designate. Prior to this time, it is possible for OCCOPS to conduct a paper review regarding some of the earlier procedural rulings. But this is the first time that anyone outside the police department, namely OCCOPS, is mandated to conduct an actual hearing into the substantive merits of the complaint. Few people in the real world are likely to have the fortitude to endure all of the police-dominated processes that must come first.

Even though the Ontario government introduced a new bill in 2006 to modify this system, the police chiefs based their arguments on what was in existence at the time they wrote.[15] Indeed, the new system is not likely to come into effect until some point in 2007. Thus, it is curious that the chiefs chose Ontario as their model. Perhaps they reckoned that, if they could make the system in Ontario sound acceptable, there could hardly be any serious criticism of the others. While there are some differences, the greatest number of complaints systems in Canada provide for the initial investigations to be done by the police themselves — not a very user-friendly way of doing things.

Even in those places with external monitoring and more accessible rights of appeal, the mere prospect of having to deal first with the police will scare off many potential complainants. At Nova Scotia's Donald Marshall Inquiry in the late 1980s, an RCMP officer revealed what is wrong with police investigating police. He explained why the RCMP pulled their punches when they reviewed the Sydney police investigation that wound up imposing twelve years of jail on Donald Marshall for a murder he did not commit: "Police officers are like a fraternity. You feel a certain loyalty to one another."[16]

If that is the case, when one police force investigates another, how much more true will it be when a police force investigates *itself*? Thus, no matter how fair, in fact, a police self-investigation might be, it cannot *appear* fair. The investigators will have collegial relations to maintain and departmental interests to protect. Inevitably, therefore, the investigating officers will have a conflict of interest. Elsewhere our society has attempted to eliminate conflicts of interest. Why should the police, of all constituencies, be treated so differently?

A number of live incidents dramatizes the defects of the current system. Consider what an external inquiry said about a Winnipeg police investigation into the role played by one of its officers in the killing of an aboriginal man: "much more attention was given to protecting [the officer] than ... to uncovering the facts."[17] In Toronto a police officer was reportedly ostracized by other members of the force after his testimony helped jail a fellow officer who had seriously assaulted a prisoner. In the result, the testifying officer resigned from the department.[18] In light of such situations, it is hard to fathom how the police chiefs and other defenders of self-investigation can still talk with a straight face.

Indeed, even if the complaints system were made more independent, that would not be good enough. In such matters, complaint-driven systems are irreparably defective. Many of those with grievances against the police will simply not file complaints. Many of them will be afraid they will not be believed. Others will fear efforts by the police to "get even."[19] Moreover, since so much counter-terrorist activity will necessarily be done in secret, many of those whose civil liberties are being abrogated may not even know it — a factor obviously fatal to the filing of complaints.

In the case of Canada's special national security agency, the Canadian Security Intelligence Service (CSIS), this problem has been reduced by the creation of the relatively independent Security Intelligence Review Committee (SIRC). With ongoing access to CSIS records, facilities, and personnel, the role of SIRC is to conduct self-generated audits of CSIS's behaviour. The results of such audits are generally publicized — a factor that can exert considerable pressure on the government. Now that the RCMP and other police forces throughout the country will be sharing the CSIS mandate insofar as terrorism is concerned, they should be similarly susceptible to the kind of audits that SIRC performs.

In this regard, the comments of former CSIS director Reid Morden are particularly noteworthy: "I remain very concerned that the new powers given to the police will not be effectively monitored and overseen to ensure that these provisions are rigorously restricted ..."[20]

Indeed, there should be independent audits of the police and of all others who are being clothed with an anti-terror mandate, for example, immigration officers and customs authorities.

Despite such warnings, the only additional oversight mechanism the government would provide is a requirement on the part of every attorney general to report the number of times the new powers of preventive detention and compulsory interrogation are used.[21] Without some kind of assessment as to the need to use these — and other — powers, numerical counts are not likely to be that helpful. Yet despite these inadequacies, Anne McLellan, the justice minister at the time, appeared to be content: "proper review and oversight ... help ensure that the [new] measures ... are applied appropriately."[22]

In the course of her testimony before the parliamentary committee, McLellan assured the MPs that the "various review mechanisms already established under Canadian law would apply to the exercise of powers under the bill."[23] She then proceeded to delineate those review mechanisms, as did the chiefs of police. But she added one they neglected to mention: "ministerial review."

THE ROLE OF THE MINISTER

Ministerial review may sound more impressive than it really is. There is a tradition in Canada that undermines the ability of cabinet ministers to supervise the police. That tradition was articulated by Pierre Trudeau, the former prime minister, in the midst of the 1970s controversy over RCMP wrongdoing: "the policy of this Government, and I believe the previous governments in this country, has been that [government] … should be kept in ignorance of the day-to-day operations of the police …"[24] Similarly, the Hughes Report on the 1997 APEC protests in Vancouver warned that the RCMP must "brook no intrusion or interference from government officials" in their "provision of security services."[25]

This doctrine of non-interference was designed to prevent the politicization of the police. The more "say" that cabinet ministers have over what the police do, the greater, it is believed, the risk will be that partisan influence will wind up controlling police behaviour. Such government involvement is seen as a short route to a police state.

Despite this obviously laudable purpose, the doctrine of non-interference creates a perplexing conundrum. Without some control over police activity, how can the civilian masters exercise responsibility for it? Canadian tradition has answered this dilemma by distinguishing operations and policies: cabinet ministers may issue general policy directives, but for the most part they should keep out of specific operations.[26]

As attractive as this may sound in theory, it could cause pimples in practice. Consider what might have happened a few years ago when the attorney general of British Columbia refused, on principle, to interfere in the RCMP handling of the aboriginal occupation at Gustafson Lake.[27] Suppose, instead of behaving with the restraint they reportedly did, the RCMP had decided to end the protest by launching a full-scale raid with overwhelming firepower. And suppose the attorney general believed that such action would have been needlessly dangerous at that time. According to some interpretations of the Canadian tradition, the minister would have been obliged to look the other way while the police perpetrated unacceptable mayhem.

In Ontario the doctrine of non-interference went even farther. Shortly after the inception of the 1995 aboriginal occupation at Ipperwash, the Ontario Provincial Police (OPP) abandoned their traditional restraint and forcibly entered the park. In the ensuing melee, an unarmed aboriginal protester was shot dead. Upon being pummelled by opposition questions in the Ontario legislature, the attorney general said: "there was no political interference ... I can only say that any political interference in the operations of the OPP would be highly inappropriate."[28] And Ontario's then premier Mike Harris further insisted: "We knew nothing of any OPP buildup. It was not our business."[29]

If, as many of Mike Harris's critics have alleged, the premier wasn't telling the truth, this situation would have been truly awful. But it might have been even worse if he *was* telling the truth. How in the world is government supposed to answer for the police if it cannot be involved in, or even know about, an operation of this magnitude?

Suppose our country embarked on potential hostilities against a comparable contingent from a foreign nation. Even if the numbers involved were the same as at Ipperwash, no one would suggest for a moment that only the military would be entitled to make such a decision. On the contrary, we would insist that the decision be made exclusively by the *government*. Why then should there be even less political involvement if we are sending 200 police officers for possible conflict with our own citizens? Imagine Janet Reno, the former U.S. attorney general, disclaiming responsibility for the raid by the Federal Bureau of Investigation (FBI) at Waco, Texas. Unlike Mike Harris, Reno could not have immunized herself with the claim that such an operation was none of her business.

From the 2005 hearings of the Maher Arar Inquiry, the public has learned of other problems connected to this Canadian doctrine of ministerial dissociation from police operations. During the cross-examination of Bill Graham, the former foreign affairs minister, there was some discussion about the fact that the minister could not be adequately briefed for certain meetings about the Arar case that involved the U.S. secretary of state.

"Do you not agree with me," the inquiry counsel asked, "that information from the RCMP or CSIS ... about what they know about Mr. Arar could have been given to you in confidence so that you could sit down with [U.S. Secretary of State] Mr. Powell on a level playing field ...?"

Graham replied, "That would require my personal engagement in operational details in a way that I think, as a minister of the crown, I think we would have to be very careful of. I would have to think about that a lot."[30]

The reply Graham gave didn't seem to satisfy his questioner. Counsel for the inquiry pressed on: "if a rookie RCMP officer who happened to be working on the file had access to that information, it would seem to me that ... a minister of the crown can also be given that information in confidence so that you can fulfill your cabinet responsibilities?"

Graham was no less insistent in his reply: "we were very limited in having operational details, and there are strong public policy reasons for that and they were respected in this case."[31]

At least in the case of Maher Arar, therefore, this doctrine helped to prevent the government of Canada from providing adequate protection for one of its citizens who haplessly fell into the custody of foreign powers. It is remarkable that the policy itself has not been more thoroughly challenged.

Moreover, why should we assume that, as between the police and the government, only the government has dubious motives of a political nature? There is no basis to believe that the police are bereft of such motives. And what about other questionable prejudices? It has been alleged, for example, that a number of police operations have been influenced by racism and homophobia within the constabulary. Why then should the appointed police be more entitled than the elected politicians to make the last mistake?

In any event, unless the government of Canada attempted to rewrite the ground rules for the interactions of police and politicians, ministerial review comes off as a rather impotent safeguard. Of course, if there were an effort to alter the relationship, the government would have to look more seriously at setting up an independent audit system. In addition to its other benefits, such a system might be needed in order to counteract any governmental propensity to let politics influence what happens. The law should require that ministerial directives to the police be issued in writing. Besides being salutary in itself, such a requirement would enable the relationship to be audited.

The government, however, made no such moves. As a result, our anti-terror law was left bereft of adequate safeguards.

5

Consequential Issues and Collateral Fallout

CONTROLLING STATUS AND MOBILITY

Revocation of Citizenship

In view of the measures Canada has adopted since 9/11, it would not be surprising if the government also sought new powers to rid this country of those persons considered to be dangerous. With few exceptions, however, the measures introduced by the government after 9/11 were identical to those it had introduced earlier. This is further evidence of Canada's long-standing deification of security.

Notwithstanding this continuity of response, it is important to examine some of the measures at issue. As always, people can lose their citizenship if they originally obtained it by perpetrating a significant deception. By itself, this provision is not remarkable. No country should feel required to recognize a claim that originated in fraud.

What is troubling, however, are some of the processes involved. Along with the citizenship bill introduced (and not passed) before 9/11, the post-9/11 bill explicitly provided that the government need prove its case only "on a balance of probabilities."[1] The risk here is that this might be interpreted to mean that people could lose their citizenship if their deception is proved on the basis of a mere preponderance of evidence. Note, for example, a difference of opinion on this subject among Canadian judges. One judge said that the revocation of citizenship required a "high degree of probability."[2] But another judge explicitly refused to adopt such an exacting burden.[3]

In a judgment rejecting such a light onus of proof, the U.S. Supreme Court declared many years ago that the revocation of citizenship is more serious than the taking of property. According to the American judges, therefore, the evidence for such purposes should be "clear, unequivocal, and convincing."[4] People don't easily pull up stakes and move from one country to another. While we should not feel obliged to honour the citizenship of those who obtained it by fraud, the burden of proof should be high. Otherwise the risk of an injustice is substantial.

Security-Related Deportations

Another problem with the procedure is the explicit denial of appeal rights in those situations where the revocation of citizenship is followed by deportation proceedings on security grounds. Once citizenship is revoked, a single federal court judge can irrevocably determine the right to stay in this country for those suspected of threatening our security. Again this could happen to someone who has endured the hardship of moving here on the strength of the permanent resident status granted by the Canadian authorities. It is arbitrary and unfair that the cosmic coincidence of drawing one judge rather than another can be allowed to resolve issues of such magnitude. At the very least there should be a right to appeal the decisions of the one judge.

Defence counsel Rocco Galati has dramatized another defect in the deportation procedures. At a deportation hearing in the late winter of 2002, Galati was representing a young man of Arab origin who had landed in Canada some six years earlier. The man was the subject of a security certificate that had been signed by the minister of immigration and solicitor general. Such certificates declare that the immigrants to whom they refer are considered threats to the security of Canada. On the basis of this certificate, deportation is authorized to the extent that a single judge of the Federal Court considers the security evaluation to be reasonable.

The rub, however, is that while the judge and government lawyer have access to the material that underlies the security certificate, neither those who are the subject of the certificate nor their lawyers are necessarily so entitled. It is possible that the only relevant material they may inspect is a sanitized summary prepared by the judge. The summary, of course, will have been denuded of details the disclosure of which is seen as jeopardizing Canada's national security.

Before the hearing in the Federal Court began, Galati solemnly announced to the judge that he intended to withdraw as the impugned man's lawyer. According to him, "it would breach the essence of my oath as a barrister to participate any further … in this process."[5] Labelling the process a "sham" and "an abomination and a breach of natural justice," Galati declared that he could not help his client when the judge and government lawyers knew the contents of the secret evidence but he and his client did not. Other prominent lawyers have expressed similar outrage. Clayton Ruby has called the procedure "a charade,"[6] and Mendel Green has referred to it as an "injustice."[7]

These defence counsel have a point. How, indeed, can they be expected to effectively represent their clients when they can't know the evidence that the judges and government lawyers know? At the same time, precarious consequences might be caused if all such material were available to all impugned immigrants and their lawyers. What happens if there are *genuine* national security considerations?

I see no reason for having to choose between the status quo and complete access to everything. In my view, and that of many reform-minded activists and lawyers, foreign nationals facing security-related deportations should be entitled to legal representation by special security-cleared public-interest advocates. Such advocates should have access to all the secret materials and they should then be mandated to advance the interests of the impugned foreign nationals at the in camera hearings of the

Federal Court. Of course, these advocates would be barred from disclosing the classified material to their "clients."

In this way, these foreign nationals could wind up with two advocates: one at the in camera hearing and one at the public hearing. The advocate at the in camera hearing would see all the material but be able to take only limited instructions. The one at the public hearing would not see all the material but could take fuller instructions. Another possibility might involve letting the impugned immigrant choose from a panel of security-cleared lawyers. This would require a special set of restrictions on lawyer-client communications.

Not a perfect system, to be sure. Perhaps not even an adequate system. I would argue, however, that such an approach would be significantly *less inadequate* than either the status quo or a system that readily revealed classified material. In this regard, I am fuelled by the comments of Paul Cavaluzzo, counsel for the Arar Inquiry. Based on his own experience as a security-cleared lawyer who cross-examined numbers of government witnesses in both secret and public hearings, Cavaluzzo has contended that this approach could serve as a model for many other types of proceedings.[8] Indeed, I believe it could be used virtually whenever classified material is being withheld from impugned persons.

There are also problems concerning the substantive grounds that can trigger deportation. Such grounds include "the subversion by force of *any* government [emphasis added]."[9] Nowhere is the elusive term *subversion* defined. Nor is the application of this provision restricted to hostile action against democracies. Suppose, therefore, permanent residents or other immigrants sent money to help foment an uprising against the government of Iran. Wouldn't such conduct amount to "the subversion by force of any government"? Do we really want to remove people from Canada for helping rid Iran and the world of the tyranny in Tehran? How else but through such "subversion" will that tyranny likely be ended?

Another problem with the substantive grounds for deportation involves mere membership in organizations suspected of terrorism.[10] Again the pivotal word *member* is nowhere defined. Not all organizations have formal dues structures. What then could count as conclusive or even acceptable evidence of membership? In many countries, organizations have a wide variety of activities and perform a number of different services. Some organizations that could be involved in terrorism also provide medical and welfare benefits. The breadth of the definitions in our law could make people deportable even if their activities inside these organizations were entirely benevolent. The danger is that some people might be removed from this country even though they did not know and/or did not approve of their organizations' terrorism.

Canadian law also authorizes deportation of immigrants who are members of an organization that "there are reasonable grounds to believe ... *will* engage in" terrorism [emphasis added].[11] Such immigrants can be forcibly removed from Canada even though they have neither done nor plotted to do anything unlawful. This is effectively deportation by clairvoyance. It is one thing to deport people for what they are doing or have done, but it risks serious injustice to make them vulnerable in this way for what anyone's crystal ball predicts they are going to do.

Here is not the place to resolve, or even to explore, how far, if at all, such risky notions as membership and prophecy should be able to authorize deportations in the case of limited visa holders and those who show up unannounced at our border. But it is the place to be more exacting at least where permanent residents are concerned. Presumably, the applications of the latter can be vetted and, if necessary, delayed until they can be vetted. But once such people pull up stakes from their home country on the basis of this country's grant of ongoing residence, it should take something more than elusive concepts to render them deportable from here. At the very least the government should feel politically impelled to demonstrate why the security of Canadians requires legislation that risks such unfairness.

Initial Withholding of Citizenship

The post-9/11 citizenship bill would have reposed a new power in the government to withhold citizenship at the outset where there are reasonable grounds to believe that a person has demonstrated a "flagrant and serious disregard for the principles and values underlying a free and democratic society."[12] As problematic as that might be, it is considerably less bad than the comparable provision that appeared in the citizenship bill introduced before 9/11. That one could have denied citizenship on the grounds that it was not "in the public interest."[13] The vagueness of this provision triggered a host of wisecracks suggesting that citizenship might be withheld from those who are less than enthusiastic about hockey.

While it must be acknowledged that different considerations might legitimately apply to the initial denial of citizenship than to its subsequent revocation, we must also appreciate the opportunities for abuse that exist even in the amended provision. In the post-9/11 bill, the federal government has the last word. There is no right of appeal or review. In view of the risks involved when those with political self-interest make these decisions, there should be some opportunity for independent review. A court should be empowered, at the very least, to determine whether the decision of the politicians is within the ballpark of reasonable judgment. As it stands, this measure creates the appearance of unfairness.

Canada's new citizenship bill contains an entirely new concept: annulment. Within five years of obtaining their citizenship, newly naturalized Canadians can have their citizenship annulled.[14] The grounds upon which that could happen include their being convicted of two summary conviction offences within a certain period before they became citizens.[15] This provision is broad enough to include camping twice without a permit. It's a wonder that the potential taboo list does not include jaywalking.

Consequential Issues and Collateral Fallout

Identity Cards

At some point in 2003, then citizenship and immigration minister Denis Coderre announced that he wished to have a debate about whether Canada should adopt a national identity card. Not surprisingly, this proposal provoked widespread criticism from privacy advocates. But Coderre stuck to his guns. At one point he responded polemically: "I hear people talk all the time about big brother and so on. They should look at the banks, the social insurance numbers, and all the databases that exist."[16] It was a little hard to understand how the existence of many current databases made it acceptable to have yet another one. Moreover, not all the examples the minister used concerned information in the hands of government. The greatest number of banks, for example, are privately owned. Isn't there a difference between having a number of databases in the private sector and enlarging those in the public sector?

At times Coderre posed the question for debate in an almost naive fashion: "Is there a way to use biometrics in a friendly manner to protect ourselves?"[17] Here the minister appeared oblivious of the problems involved in an ID card. Of course, the whole point of an ID card with identifiers is to enhance our security. To that extent, the proposed measure would be "friendly." But such comments ignore the fact that the very measure that would protect our security would simultaneously reduce our autonomy.

Indeed, the issue of ID cards represents a classic dilemma. At some point, measures adopted to serve some values can wind up hurting other ones. That is what civil liberties problems are typically all about. In the case of identity cards in particular, there are real questions whether the amount of security obtained would be worth the loss of autonomy sustained.

It is one thing to provide for biometric identifiers in documents such as passports or licences whose primary purpose is to facilitate particular activities such as international travel or automobile driving. It is another thing entirely to use such identifiers to facilitate movement — or even to justify being — anywhere

within Canada. Moreover, it is hard to imagine how such identifiers would likely improve this country's security unless they
became part of a national database. To what extent, therefore, was
Coderre considering any measure that would require everyone
within the country to provide the government with fingerprints
and/or retinal identifiers?

During the course of his discussions, the minister suggested
that ID cards might be used on a voluntary basis. If so, it is then
hard to imagine how much security they could possibly provide.
On the other hand, it is probable that a mandatory system would
be exceptionally intrusive. Such compulsion would not likely provide the contemplated security unless everyone were required at
all times to carry the ID card. That could mean, of course, creating a criminal offence simply for the failure to have the card available when the authorities asked to see it. To what extent could
such demands be made of pedestrians on the street and even residents in their homes?

Such concerns are frequently expressed by experts in the field.
According to University of Maryland professor Ben Shneiderman,
for example, "a national ID system requires an extensive database of
personal information on every citizen."[18] And Stanford University
law professor Tom Campbell, a former California member of the
U.S. Congress, declared, "if you have an ID card, it is solely for the
purpose of allowing the government to compel you to produce it."[19]
Similarly, Ed Crane, president of the Cato Institute, warned that
"we shouldn't be forced to show our papers wherever we go."[20]

In response to those who consider such comments to be
groundless scare-mongering, consider a survey conducted by
Privacy International. It found that "police who are given powers
to demand ID invariably have consequent powers to detain people who do not have the card and cannot prove their identity."[21]
Indeed, according to Privacy International, "even in such
advanced countries as Germany, the power to hold such people
for up to 24 hours is enshrined in law."[22] In this way, a national
identity card could well wind up reducing the freedoms of *completely innocent* people.

The question is whether the gains outweigh the losses. There are reasons to doubt it. A not insignificant factor is the relative lack of enthusiasm in the law-enforcement community. In the United Kingdom, for example, the Association of Chiefs of Police Officers has said that while it is in favour of a voluntary system, its members would be reluctant to administer a compulsory card because it might erode relations with the public.[23] Similar sentiments were expressed by Dutch police authorities.[24]

If a national identity card were considered so important for the protection of national security, one would expect law-enforcement agencies to be salivating to get it. Imagine police departments being willing to undergo a reduction in their power to search, seize, and arrest in order to accommodate public relations! In this regard, it is significant to note that the British officials who briefed Canada's relevant parliamentary committee declared that the contemplated ID card in the United Kingdom "would not be a particularly useful tool …" to address national security issues, such as terrorism.[25]

Moreover, there is no reason to be complacently confident about the state of the technology, since "for a card to be highly secure, the committee was told that there will have to be a lot of false rejects,"[26] that is, false positives. The more false rejects there are, the more legitimate ID card holders will be subject to suspicion and accusations. According to witnesses who appeared before the committee, the lowering of the false reject rate would result in raising the false accept rate. But, as the committee also noted, that would undermine the very purpose of creating a national identity card.[27]

There is also no reason to be sanguine about the risks of fraud and forgery. An article in *USA Today* reported: "Gone are the crude, cut-and-paste fake IDs common a few years ago that were so obviously bogus. They have been replaced with replicas whose detail and accuracy often astonish authorities …"[28]

Such risks are exacerbated by the inevitable need to base a national identity card on certain "foundation documents." To whatever extent, for example, a birth certificate or driver's licence is forged, the consequent national identity card would also be compromised.

In this regard, the parliamentary committee stated that "the risk of fraudulently obtained foundation documents is real and could jeopardize a multi-billion dollar national identity card system."[29] There is an old adage: garbage in, garbage out. As the committee noted, a compromised ID card system could actually make life easier for terrorists "because they could use their ID cards while security personnel would concentrate on those without one."[30]

Not to be outdone as a defender of privacy, Coderre insisted that "the biggest threat to individual privacy is to have one's identity stolen and used by someone else."[31] According to the National Research Council in the United States, however, "it is likely that the existence of a single, distinct source of identity would create a single point of failure that could *facilitate* identity theft [emphasis added]."[32]

Also unsettling is the fact that "virtually all ID cards worldwide develop a broader usage over time than was originally envisioned for them."[33] Moreover, we cannot afford to be complacent about how securely our personal data will be managed. According to Privacy International, even in government "it is generally assumed that at any one time, one percent of staff will be willing to sell or trade confidential information for personal gain."[34] Thus, in many respects, a national identity card begins to look more like a threat than a hope. In any event, there is reason to believe that such cards are a long distance from what they are cracked up to be.

TORTURE

The American Cracks in the Anti-Torture Consensus

Earlier I alluded to the exposé in the spring of 2004 of how U.S. soldiers had humiliated and intimidated Iraqi prisoners they were holding in a Baghdad jail. The one redeeming feature in this sad saga of American misbehaviour is the universal condemnation that it provoked in every sector of American society. There were virtually no exceptions. Everybody who was anybody denounced the culpable American soldiers.

Unfortunately, the nobility of this response was soon seriously undermined. A few weeks after the Baghdad exposé, something else came to light: an internal memorandum to U.S. defence secretary Donald Rumsfeld, prepared by a team of lawyers at the Pentagon. The memorandum purported to provide a legal justification for the use of torture by the president of the United States.[35]

The sweep of the document was particularly unnerving. Invoking the president's "complete authority over the conduct of war," the memo justified overriding the Geneva Conventions, an international treaty against torture, and U.S. federal laws that explicitly banned torture. Indeed, the memo argued that such laws "must be construed as inapplicable to interrogations undertaken pursuant to [the president's] commander-in-chief authority."[36]

And though this was more than enough to let the president do just about anything he wanted, note how high the memo set the threshold for torture: "the infliction of pain or suffering per se ... is insufficient to amount to torture." The pain had to be "severe" and "of such a high level of intensity" that it resembles organ failure, impairment of bodily functions, or "even death."[37]

One of the most disquieting consequences of this document was the damage it caused to the universal consensus in the civilized world. According to a United Nations convention, there are "no exceptional circumstances whatsoever ... [that] may be invoked as a justification of torture."[38] Similar admonitions are contained in the Universal Declaration of Human Rights and the International Covenant on Civil and Political Rights.[39] It appears, therefore, that the U.S. government opened a veritable Pandora's box.

Vulnerable Arguments Against Torture

To the extent that those critical of this U.S. initiative based their arguments on moral grounds, they made a compelling case. After all, torture represents a grievous assault on the commitment of the democracies to the ideal of equal human dignity. The democracies must, therefore, treat everyone, even their enemies, with fundamental dignity. It is hard to imagine an activity more ethically incompatible with the philosophy of democracy than the deliberate infliction of pain. The immorality of torture is as close to self-evident as anything can be.

But when the critics began to use *prudential* arguments, fallacies in their logic soon surfaced. According to Kenneth Roth of Human Rights Watch, the acceptance of the legal advice in the Pentagon memorandum would give to "dictators world-wide ... a ready-made excuse to ignore one of the most basic prohibitions of international human-rights law."[40] The *Globe and Mail* echoed these sentiments: "If the United States can claim [the right to torture] so can any number of tyrannies."[41]

These comments seem to assume that, until the advent of the Pentagon memo, the dictators of this world were scrupulously avoiding the use of torture. That would indeed be news to those hapless people who wound up in the jails of Saddam's Iraq, the ayatollahs' Iran, Assad's Syria, the Taliban's Afghanistan, Communist China, and Communist North Korea, to name only a few. Nor is there any reason to believe that the world's terrorists have been influenced by the anti-torture posture that America had adopted until this point. No matter how disquieted we legitimately are as a result of the Pentagon's unsettling memorandum, we damage our cause by invoking these fallacious arguments.

As contended earlier, the inconsistencies that people commit do not necessarily impugn the validity of all the positions they adopt. But when commentators contradict themselves, they can hurt the *political* credibility of their cause. Although the torturers of this world never needed encouragement from the United States, American resort to such tactics threatens to reduce America's political ability to exert anti-torture pressures.

By the same token, the anti-torture crusade becomes less saleable in the hands of those who support capital punishment. A number of President Bush's critics in the U.S. Democratic Party, for example, have fallen into this trap.

Consequential Issues and Collateral Fallout

What kind of policy says that it is wrong to wound but right to kill? The relevant U.N. convention, supported by many such critics of the Bush administration, forbids "any act by which severe pain or suffering, whether physical or mental, is intentionally inflicted on a person" in order to obtain information.[42] Conceivably, however, if a state inflicts the pain of death and its anticipation, not to obtain information but to exact punishment, no such violation will have been committed. As a result, we are left with a strange paradox: lethal torture may be inflicted after it is too late to help the victims, but non-lethal torture may not be inflicted in time to save the victims. (In view of the fact that it is possible to impose sufficiently long and effective imprisonment, including life in maximum security, I discount the argument that execution is needed to prevent murderers from murdering again.)

Problems in the Moral Absolutist Position

Having dealt with these prudential arguments concerning torture, I return now to questions of morality. As indicated, I believe that the moral arguments are the most compelling. Does this mean, however, that exceptions are out of the question? Must the position be absolute?

Consider a genuine "ticking-bomb" situation. To test the limits of our taboo, take an extreme case. Suppose our police or intelligence agencies learned that a nuclear device had been planted in the heart of a large Canadian city. And suppose there were strong grounds to believe that Mr. X knew the location of the device but refused to disclose it. If there was also a strong basis to anticipate that a nuclear explosion was only hours away, to what extent should our moral opposition to torture remain intact?

Unless the foregoing scenario is considered virtually impossible, we may have to decide whether there are *any* circumstances that could morally justify torture. In view of what the al-Qaeda terrorists have already perpetrated and what we have every reason to believe they would like to do in the future, it would be a mistake to dismiss such a development out of hand. Moreover, it is not reasonable to believe that they could *never* have the ability to acquire weapons of mass destruction.

At this point it is necessary to revisit the issue of what exactly constitutes torture. After all, incarceration itself creates enormous suffering. Yet as long as those to be jailed are treated with procedural fairness, few would deny the legitimacy of such punishment. Nor is it necessary, of course, for the facilities of a prison to emulate those of a luxury hotel. But the *deliberate* infliction of pain or discomfort is another story. According to Claudio Cordone, the legal director of Amnesty International, "sleep deprivation, prolonged standing, uncomfortable positions, shackling — all amount to ill-treatment and torture as well."[43] So, too, according to Human Rights Watch, does the use of sodium pentothal or truth serum.[44] All of that, of course, sets the bar much lower than what is advocated in the Pentagon memorandum.

In any event, it is virtually certain that in most democracies the intentional creation of pain more severe than the foregoing would qualify as torture. This could include psychological as well as physical suffering. According to one expert, for example, "it's very common [in some places] for a prisoner to be told that they're bringing his wife and children in. He'll hear screams or cries next door."[45] Such practices, all too common in countries with authoritarian governments, have long been condemned in the democratic West, including until recently the United States.

To be more accurate, some cracks in the West began to appear earlier. In the late winter of 2003, the capture of an upper-echelon official of al-Qaeda triggered a serious debate in North America about the ethical permissibility of torture. The willingness to reconsider long-held values and beliefs derived, in large part, from the contribution made by eminent Harvard law professor Alan Dershowitz, a widely renowned civil libertarian. He suggested the need to take a fresh look at the possibility of legalized torture. The eminence of his reputation and the cogency of his arguments simply could not be ignored.

In Canada the *Globe and Mail* took up the challenge. First the newspaper published a piece by Dershowitz himself. This was followed by an article from William Schulz, the American director of Amnesty International; a host of letters to the editor; and an official editorial. The overwhelming response to the Dershowitz approach was negative.[46] The arguments, however, were not persuasive.

According to Amnesty's Schulz, the acceptance of so repugnant a practice as torture "is an invitation to chaos."[47] Unquestionably, the risk of such chaos would be considerable. But nowhere did Schulz consider the possible chaos that could accompany the *failure* to inflict torture. In view of what we know about Hiroshima and Nagasaki, we can now readily imagine the kind of devastation that would occur if that "ticking bomb" in the middle of a large city were to ignite. Doesn't the argument require a comparison of chaotic outcomes?

The American Amnesty director correctly challenged the assumption that our authorities could know for a moral certainty that any candidate for torture possessed the relevant information.[48] He contended that it is difficult to tell ahead of time who has such information and who does not. In this regard, he reminded us that more than a hundred innocent people in the United States have been convicted of capital crimes and sentenced to death despite all of the legal protections and safeguards of the American court system.

If such awful miscarriages could occur after a trial, how many more might happen without it? In view of the wrongful murder convictions suffered by Donald Marshall, Guy Paul Morin, and David Milgaard within a short period of time, Canadians have no reason to feel significantly more sanguine than the Americans about the ability of the authorities here to make these kinds of judgments.

But in so many situations far less drastic than those involving a ticking nuclear device, our justice system continues constantly to make such anticipatory decisions. Indeed, the system would not be able to function adequately *unless* it could make at least some such judgments. Consider the decisions that are made every day as to whether a suspect will be freed or jailed *before* trial. Our courts are explicitly mandated to determine in advance the likelihood that accused persons will abscond or commit crimes if they are released on bail.

Few seriously question the acceptability of the power to impose periods of incarceration (not infrequently weeks) even though the accused people have not been convicted of the offences at issue. For such purposes, our justice system believes it is enough that there are reasonable grounds to believe that the accused person is likely to misbehave if allowed to roam free. No analogy, of course, quite fits the catastrophic circumstances envisioned in the hypothetical scenario involving torture to prevent a nuclear holocaust. The analogies might serve, however, to ensure that the possibility of error will not necessarily trump all other considerations.

One approach frequently invoked by certain opponents of torture is to deny its effectiveness. According to this argument, it is patently immoral to employ so repugnant a tactic unless you are reasonably sure that it is going to work. What could be more immoral than the *gratuitous* infliction of pain? Thus, for example, Tom Malinowski of Human Rights Watch contended that "torture is a wonderful technique for getting confessions from innocent people and a lousy technique for getting truth out of guilty people."[49] Similarly, a former deputy director of the FBI conceded that "people will even admit that they killed their grandmother, just to stop the beatings."[50]

Physical coercion, however, has been used not only to extract confessions, but also to acquire information. For these purposes, it is not so clear that such tactics could *never* work. A confession, even a false one, could put a halt to the application of physical pressure. But where information is the objective, the pressure could be revived if a disclosure proved to be inaccurate. Dershowitz claims, for instance, that in 1995 the Philippine authorities coerced a terrorist into disclosing information "that may have foiled plots to assassinate the Pope and to crash 11 commercial airlines carrying approximately 4,000 passengers into the Pacific Ocean, as well as a plan to fly a private Cessna filled with explosives into CIA headquarters."[51]

I suspect that the refusal of many commentators to ease up on the anti-torture taboo has less to do with the above considerations than with the myriad of other scenarios that any let-up would make possible. What may be of concern is the slippery slope: permit torture in one situation and inevitably it will be applied to others. This fear is not without justification. Experience has demonstrated time and again the susceptibility of our legal powers to misuse and abuse.

Indeed, as noted above, the *Globe and Mail* debate about torture was precipitated not by the fear of an imminent nuclear explosion, but by the capture of a pivotal al-Qaeda official. At the time of the capture there was no particular evidence that al-Qaeda was plotting to use, or that it even possessed, weapons of mass destruction. If such speculative possibilities could undo the anti-torture taboo of a stalwart civil libertarian like Alan Dershowitz, how much more would likely be uncorked if we decided to move in this direction?

No doubt such considerations prompted Amnesty's William Schulz to warn "how quickly officially authorized torture would diminish the credibility" of the war on terrorism. "How many people," he asked, "would need to be tortured before our allies threw up their hands in disgust ...?"[52] Similarly, the *Globe and Mail* editorial declared that "when we allow our bedrock values to be eroded, we have already lost the very thing we are so desperate to defend ... once the taboo against torture falls, what next?"[53]

All of these are legitimate concerns, but the nagging possibility remains: suppose we were to face a real ticking-bomb situation. Could we possibly allow the fear of what might happen at another time prevent us from taking the requisite action at the time in question? According to Schulz, "the ticking-bomb scenario in its purest form is a fantasy of 'moral' torture all too easily appropriated by tyrants."[54] Yes, such scenarios can be readily exploited by tyrants, but in the dangerous world of post-9/11 we can no longer indulge the notion that the scenario is merely fantasy.

I have expended the effort here to assess the arguments of these anti-torture advocates not because I disagree with their

ultimate conclusions, but because I agree with them. I fear, however, that they have not taken the most persuasive route to their
desirable destination. Alan Dershowitz is a formidable advocate;
his tough-minded analysis requires a tough-minded response.
That, in my view, is what is largely missing from the foregoing
criticisms of his position. The ensuing comments are my
attempt to plug this loophole.

In his book *Why Terrorism Works*, Dershowitz uses one argument that appears unanswerable: "The real issue ... is not whether
some torture would or would not be used in the ticking bomb
case — it would. The question is whether it would be done openly, pursuant to a previously established legal procedure, or
whether it would be done ... in violation of existing law."[55]

Of course, it is hard to imagine that, faced with a real ticking
nuke, the authorities in our society would not resort to virtually
any tactic that they thought would work. What must be
addressed, therefore, is Dershowitz's idea that we should establish
in advance a legal regime for torture.

The Torture Warrant Fallacy

In Alan Dershowitz's view, we should consider empowering our
judges to issue what amounts to "torture warrants" in circumstances where they believe that the prescribed conditions prevail.[56] He appears to believe that the requirement to obtain judicial warrants would decrease the number of times our society
wound up using torture.

I am not so sure. Consider what such a law would say. It
might provide, for example, that a court could grant a torture
warrant in the face of an imminent peril of monumental proportions. Even if the word *imminent* is precise enough, what about
monumental proportions or any similar expression? Would the
threat have to encompass millions of lives? What about thousands, or hundreds, or dozens? Of course, the law could specify
that the threat had to be nuclear. But would that be rational? After
all, if the prospect of a nuke could loosen the legal restrictions

against torture, why not the threat of a chemical or biological attack? They are capable of wiping out masses of people and they could deliver substantial suffering to boot. So could more conventional instruments that are located in, or rammed into, critical places, such as happened in the case of 9/11.

On the other hand, suppose that fewer lives were imperilled, but the circumstances were particularly wrenching. What about a kidnapping where a handful of innocent people were facing imminent decapitation? If someone in our custody knew where the hostages were and refused to reveal it, would this situation be so different in substance from the example of a pending nuclear explosion? If the rationale is to save innocent lives from the imminent peril of a horrible death, why should numbers be such a critical factor? And if all of these circumstances could justify torture, one might ask why the horribleness of the death should be so critical. Shouldn't our society be prepared to take exceptional steps to save innocent people from *any* unwelcome death?

Or suppose the information at issue was the hiding place of Osama bin Laden. The disclosure of his whereabouts might not avert an "imminent" peril, but it could conceivably cripple a particularly dangerous network of terrorist operations. Such an outcome could well save a great many innocent lives. With any flexibility in the language of the applicable statute, a judicial warrant for torture might well be forthcoming in these circumstances.

In such ways, a legal power to torture could steadily expand. To stop it, the governing statute would have to employ exceptionally narrow criteria. But what would they be? As noted, it would seem irrational to confine the operative circumstances to those involving extremely large numbers of people or particularly horrible deaths. No matter how the criteria were spelled out, every judicial warrant would become a precedent for the next one. Step by step, the range of permissible torture could grow. Each increase would flow logically from the last one. It is highly probable, therefore, that legalization would produce torture in situations a substantial distance from those that were originally envisioned.

And how certain would we need to be that any candidate for torture actually knew the information we were seeking? A certainty of 100 percent would be unrealistically demanding. Indeed, there is virtually no such thing. But how much less would be tolerable — 90 percent, 80 percent, 70 percent? At best such calculations would be hopelessly inexact. Moreover, to what extent would it be necessary to believe that any candidates for torture were themselves complicit in terrorist activity? What about an innocent person who knew where the bombs or hostages were but refused to talk not because of any personal culpability, but because the terrorists had threatened to kidnap his children?

It is important to remember that if the threat were really imminent there would be precious little time for a patient, meticulous hearing to sort out all these issues. It is likely that any such hearings would be rushed or perhaps even slipshod — not the kind of procedure that should invest an act of torture with a judicial imprimatur.

Moreover, the mere act of legalizing torture could have a transformative effect on our society. We would have to consider what methods are acceptable under what circumstances. The resulting parliamentary debate is a nightmare to contemplate. Would it be permissible to crush a testicle or gouge an eye? Dershowitz has already talked about the less-damaging — but no less painful — treatment of jabbing under fingernails.

We would probably also feel the need to choose in advance the persons who would administer the pain. Just imagine the consequent job interviews. What kind of curriculum vitae would potential applicants require? The entire process of establishing the requisite machinery would debase the kind of civilization we had hoped that we had become.

It should, therefore, be clear how wrong it would be to legalize torture.

Is There a Less Unacceptable Alternative?

If our society really did face an imminent catastrophe, would we then be left with virtually no option but prayer? As Alan

Dershowitz has already argued, the authorities would likely resort to extraordinary measures no matter what the law said. If the peril were sufficiently great, imminent, and obvious, the risk of torture would commensurately increase.

The issue then is how to respond. In the interests of preserving a viable rule of law, there must be no suggestion *in advance* that such torture will elicit a special response. As long as torture remains unlawful, as I have argued it must, it should be treated like any other crime. That is, anyone who employs it will be subject to the ordeals of investigation, arrest, prosecution, adjudication, and incarceration.

But this does not necessarily rule out some leniency in a sufficiently dire emergency. Indeed, a sound system of justice must always allow for both tough and soft responses. We can choose, for example, not to prosecute. After all, prosecutorial discretion is a traditional prerogative of the Crown. Alternatively, even if we do prosecute, the courts should remain empowered to impose lighter penalties as well as harsher ones, depending on their view of the circumstances. This means, of course, that mandatory minimum sentences must be abolished.

In any event, these are decisions that should be made only *after* the fact, not beforehand. Thus, those who decide to inflict torture must have no advance guarantees. Only in that way will it be meaningful to maintain torture as an unlawful act. Such a response would apply even to the police officer who physically coerces a prisoner into identifying the location of a bomb and to the father who beats an accomplice into disclosing the whereabouts of his kidnapped child. Many people may well believe that, in such circumstances, assaults are morally acceptable or at least socially excusable.

For their sake, we should retain the right to be lenient. But in the interests of avoiding the slippery slope of Dershowitz's warrant-granting scheme, we must also retain the option to be harsh. Thus, any persons who resort to torture will know they are incurring a significant risk of serious legal consequences.

Admittedly, this solution is not a happy one. The fact is, however, there is no happy solution. Given the dangers of legalization on the one hand and undue rigidity on the other, I can only argue that the foregoing represents the *least bad* of the alternative possibilities. One of the most disturbing outcomes of 9/11 is that this grotesque subject has made it at all to the political agenda of the Western democracies.

A WORD ABOUT U.S. DOMESTIC BEHAVIOUR

In the fall of 2003, Canadians were shocked over the allegations made by one of their fellow citizens, Syrian-born Maher Arar. A year earlier he had been intercepted in New York on his return from a trip abroad. U.S. authorities detained him for several days, subjected him to a lengthy interrogation without the assistance of counsel, and finally deported him to his native Syria where he was imprisoned for many months. During this incarceration, Arar was frequently beaten and tortured by his Syrian captors. Shortly after his release and return to Canada, he held a press conference in which he described his ordeal in some grisly detail.[57]

In certain ways, the most disquieting aspect of his story occurred in a subsequent meeting between Canada's then solicitor general Wayne Easter and then U.S. attorney general John Ashcroft. At that meeting Ashcroft reportedly defended the propriety of what the American authorities had done. As far as he was concerned, they had every right to pack Arar off to Syria.[58] The fact that he was a Canadian citizen travelling on a Canadian passport apparently failed to impress the United States. Nor did Ashcroft appear even slightly embarrassed by the widespread suspicion that the Americans did it in order to extract information from Arar that they were unable to get. In short, the suspected purpose of the exercise was to facilitate the very torture that Arar ultimately suffered.

Although Canadians were sympathetic with America's post-9/11 determination to fight terrorism on all fronts, there was considerable concern over Ashcroft's attitude. Did U.S. law really permit that American action? Even so did the Americans have no qualms about inflicting such treatment on the citizen of a fellow democracy and long-time ally? And had torture become an acceptable component of American behaviour?

Such questions served to exacerbate the anxiety many Canadians were feeling about American conduct in other situations. What were the Americans going to do with the hundreds of prisoners they had captured from the battlefields of Afghanistan? Since their capture, many of these prisoners were being held at the U.S. base in Guantánamo, Cuba.[59] Then there was the bizarre case of José Padilla, a U.S. citizen who had been arrested not on a foreign battlefield, but in Chicago, Illinois. All of these prisoners were being held without ready access to the remedial role of the courts.[60]

These actions were being taken under the presumed authority of U.S. President George W. Bush. As the commander-in-chief responsible for protecting Americans from the danger of terrorism, Bush simply declared that all of these prisoners, including Padilla, were enemy combatants; therefore, they could not avail themselves of the instruments of U.S. justice.[61]

It seemed quite incredible that, on the basis of nothing more than executive fiat, the noble protections of the U.S. Constitution could be so blithely overridden. As for the foreign nationals who had been seized in Afghanistan, there was at least an argument. After all, they had been taken in battle. There had never been a serious suggestion that such "due process" rights be extended to the German and Japanese soldiers who had been captured in World War II. On the other hand, the earlier prisoners could avail themselves of the protections in the Hague Convention — a remedy Bush has not generally honoured. Moreover, terrorism is a continuing danger. To release at least some of these prisoners is to run the risk that they will return to inflict the very harm they were prevented from causing in the first place.

A critical difference obtains, however, between the wars of the past and the one in the present. The other wars came to definitive and discernible conclusions. But the war against terrorism could well extend indefinitely into the future — perhaps even in perpetuity. The necessary implication of George W. Bush's position is that it might become permissible to incarcerate these prisoners for the rest of their lives. Quite a policy for the leader of the democratic world to adopt.

As far as Padilla is concerned, Bush can't invoke the arguments that might apply to those captured in Afghanistan. Padilla, as I have said, was not arrested on any foreign battlefield. He was arrested in the continental United States. Furthermore, he is an American citizen. For the president unilaterally to label him an enemy combatant is effectively to jettison the U.S. Bill of Rights. Something simply has to give. Even those suspected of terrorism must receive some level of independent adjudication.[62]

This issue was followed by a *New York Times* revelation that, in the aftermath of 9/11, President Bush had unilaterally authorized electronic surveillance against American residents within the United States.[63] Again people wondered why the president bypassed the statutory requirement that he obtain judicial warrants for such intrusive snooping. After all, since 9/11, the special U.S. court on national security matters had rejected government warrant applications in only four of more than 5,000 cases.[64] Moreover, the American statute permits *warrantless* bugging for three days in urgent circumstances.[65] Even accepting the government's argument that the special court modified, rather than dismissed, more of these warrant applications, the White House acknowledged that this happened in only 3 percent of the cases.[66]

As of the end of 2005, no apologies were forthcoming from the U.S. government. On the contrary, there was an announcement of a probe to determine who had leaked the information to the press. Even if President Bush believed that he had the constitutional power in these circumstances to act unilaterally, it was especially hard — in the absence of a fuller explanation — to fathom why he would do it. In view of all the anti-American feeling that has been generated since the Iraq war, this presidential behaviour appeared to represent a *gratuitous* departure from the principles of civil liberties that the Americans claim to champion.

RELIGIOUS FAITH AND SECULAR CLOUT

The Nature of the Religious Challenge

A central component of our society's conflict with terrorism is ideological. In certain key respects, I am afraid we may not be up to it.

To the terrorists of al-Qaeda, the West represents the infidels. Al-Qaeda's mission comes from Allah, that is, from God. When they fly planes into our buildings, seize our innocent civilians, and detonate bombs in our hotel lobbies, they believe they are obeying the Will of God. What do we have that can match that?

There is no shortage of people on our side who also profess to follow the Will of God. And significant numbers of them are even prepared to have our public policy influenced, if not governed, by the Divine Will as they understand it. In the United States, the religious Right has become a formidable force. Politicians ignore them at their peril. Indeed, they have even been able to claim certain presidents as adherents, for example, Ronald Reagan and George W. Bush. As indicated earlier, Bush reportedly contended at one point that he was told by God Himself to hit al-Qaeda and Saddam.

In Canada this phenomenon is not as dominant, but it is hardly nonexistent. Significant elements of the Canadian Alliance, now part of the new Conservative Party, claimed to rely on Divine guidance in the formation of their policies. (Remember the earlier Stockwell Day?) One political party, the Christian Heritage Party, regularly invokes the Will of God as the authority to resolve political disputes. Arguing, for instance, that pornography is an offence "both against humankind and God," this party has advocated "tighter censorship."[67]

On the issue of abortion, the Christian Heritage Party has also invoked the Will of God as have other fundamentalist groups such as the Evangelical Fellowship of Canada.[68] In addition, the abortion issue has attracted the substantial involvement of the Roman Catholic Church. In a 1998 statement, an affiliated organization, the Society for Catholic Life and Culture, included a reference to the authority of God: "We ... proclaim the intrinsic evil of abortion, direct sterilization, and contraception. Those evils are so clearly a denial of God's love that no circumstances can render them licit."[69]

On numerous occasions, those opposing gay rights have also relied on the Deity. When the leaders of certain gay groups were introduced to the Alberta legislature, Stockwell Day reportedly characterized the event as "an offence against the Lord."[70] Expressing its opposition to a Supreme Court decision granting spousal benefits to homosexual couples, the Christian Heritage Party said: "If the word 'supremacy' has any meaning, it means that God's revealed condemnation of homosexual unions must be respected in all Canadian legislation and judicial rulings. That precludes giving legal sanction and protection to what God has declared to be wrong."[71]

In fairness I feel obliged to point out that this propensity to invoke God emanates not only from the religious Right, but also from its Left. Consider the following remarks made by mainstream Canadian church leaders on the subject of nuclear weapons: "We can conceive of no circumstances under which the use of nuclear weapons could be … consistent with the Will of God, and we must therefore conclude that nuclear weapons must therefore be rejected as a means of threat or deterrence."[72] These church leaders quoted with approval an American clergyman who had said, "it is a sin not merely to use, or merely to threaten to use, but merely to build and to possess nuclear weapons."[73]

I have not reproduced all of these references in order to encourage any increase of such religious involvement in our public life. In my view, the Western democracies would not be strengthened against the theocrats of al-Qaeda by counterposing them to the theocrats on our side. We cannot persuasively answer them by insisting that we know God's Will better than they do.

Our claim to ideological superiority in this conflict requires us, as a collectivity, to eschew such invocation of the Deity. The best response to their arrogant claims of knowing God's Will is our humble acknowledgement that we are bereft of such knowledge. As democratic societies, we accommodate a wide range of beliefs on such matters within our collective bosom. Thus, many individual members of the Western democracies have a wide range of beliefs concerning God and God's Will. But what distinguishes us from the kind of mentality found in al-Qaeda is a refusal to use force or coercion to further anyone's beliefs in that regard.

A key reason to reject compulsion in such matters is the impossibility of relating to anything as Divinely willed without becoming mired in a hopeless dilemma. If a command, commandment, or policy direction comes from God, it cannot logically be questioned or challenged. How can perfection be subject to human question and challenge? But *we* are finite mortals. Hence, we must question and challenge all of our beliefs. Since we might be wrong, we must question what we believe. As soon as we do, we are no longer *treating* the objects of our belief *as though* they came from God. They cannot be subject to and beyond question at the same time. To deny that what we believe is open to challenge is effectively to affirm that we cannot be wrong on the subject at issue. That would become an exercise in *self*-idolatry — a sin to all theocrats.

Moreover, how is a mere mortal supposed to recognize God in the event of a communication or revelation? There are no logical axioms or scientific principles by which we can do it. It is a matter of our subjective intuitions. But how can we trust *them* to make judgments of such enormity? Humans would not know an absolute if they fell over one. This observation applies not only to the fallible human beings we know in this century, but also even to those from antiquity whose reported encounters with God the theocrats of this century rely upon.

Consider the classic case of the Bible's Abraham. When he got the command to kill his son, Isaac, how did he know that the voice he heard belonged to God? Wasn't it just as plausible to impute such a horrible command to the Devil or even to his own imagination? Furthermore, how did he know that he got the message straight? Couldn't there have been a "not" that he did not hear?

"Faith" is the answer we will get from many quarters. But faith in whom and in what? In order for Abraham to obey such an awful command, the faith he had to have was not necessarily in God; it was in *himself.* He had to believe in his own ability to identify the source and contents of that horrible command.

There is no way that we finite earthlings can avoid this dilemma. Who can we trust as the authentic recipient of God's word? The pope, ayatollah, primate, or rabbi? Since they disagree with one another, their claims cannot all be equally valid. We have also had the experience where the likes of Sirhan Sirhan, Charles Manson, and the Son of Sam tell us they were acting under Divine instructions when they committed their terrible crimes. On what basis do we deny their claims? Morality? Normative tradition? The Ten Commandments?

Such replies won't wash. We cannot tie God to our standards of right and wrong. Our morality is supposed to derive its legitimacy because it comes from Him, not the other way around. Thus, there is no basis upon which we can deny the possibility that God could countermand any of His earlier revealed injunctions. Moreover, God, being perfect, might appear, according to our finite perceptions, to behave inconsistently and He might decide to withhold His reasons from us. We cannot impose our standards on the absolute. There are simply no criteria by which we can test revelation claims. We are stuck with our finite, subjective, intuitive faculties. Again we cannot with consistency allow *them* to be the judge of what is absolute.

This is not to denigrate the important role that has been played by the world's great religions. I am questioning neither the claim that there is a God nor the validity of religious beliefs. I am simply questioning the exercise of applying them to public policy. In a pluralistic world of colliding values, we have no way of divining the Divine Will without reposing absolutist faith in our own powers of discernment or in that of any human recipients of claimed revelations. Either way it is too much for finite mortals.

It is to the everlasting credit of the Western democracies that they have, at least implicitly, acknowledged the inescapability of these dilemmas and have foresworn the use of violence or coercion to further anyone's — even the majority's — finite, subjective intuitions. Similarly, it is to the everlasting shame of the theocrats in al-Qaeda that they are willing, even eager, to wantonly slaughter innocent people in order to implement their finite, subjective intuitions.

The centrality of ideology to our current struggle requires an ongoing effort to buttress the integrity of our position. Hypocrisy and inconsistency have the capacity to undermine the viability of what we profess to be fighting for. Regrettably, such elements are all too common in today's Canada. From the standpoint of democratic norms, there are too many forces that would excessively promote — but inadequately protect — religious belief and observance. The situations that I am about to describe are designed to persuasively illustrate, rather than definitively delineate, the existence of this phenomenon.

Excessive Promotion of Religion

Canadian society has been embroiled in a dispute over whether to legitimate same-sex marriage. Weighing in against such legitimation is the Interfaith Coalition on Marriage and Family, comprised of the Islamic Society of North America, the Catholic Civil Rights League, and the Evangelical Fellowship of Canada. In papers filed before the Supreme Court of Canada, the coalition argued that, by altering the conception of marriage in order to recognize same-sex unions, "Parliament would be failing to manifest equal concern for the interests of the members of the religious faith communities represented by the Interfaith Coalition as well as other Canadians, who will be marginalized from full participation in civil society."[74]

The magnitude of the non sequitur here is simply breathtaking. If gay marriage were to acquire a status equal to straight marriage, how in the world would that render the religious believers represented by this coalition *less* equal members of society? And how in the world would it marginalize them from full participation in civil society? On the basis of this logic, the abolition of slavery in the United States marginalized white Americans. And the granting of full civil rights to Jews marginalized Gentiles. In the foregoing examples, perhaps it might be argued that racists and anti-Semites had lost something. For those who are prepared to live and let live, however, no such loss would have been sustained.

The Interfaith Coalition has an important question to answer: why *should* the law of a democratic society be tailored for those who are *not* prepared to live and let live?

As of the early 1990s, the Ontario Court of Appeal invalidated religious exercises and instruction in the Ontario public school system.[75] According to the court, these practices violated religious freedom and equality as guaranteed by the Charter of Rights and Freedoms. In a number of provinces, however, the school systems have been constitutionally immunized from the application of the Charter. Not infrequently, such immunization is attributable to the legal terms by which the province in question joined Confederation. Take the situation in Alberta. A number of classrooms there are slated to begin with the recitation of the Lord's Prayer. The governing statute also provides that public school boards in that province *may* prescribe religious instruction and exercises for their students.[76]

While it is difficult to determine exactly how many such school boards authorize — and how many schools actually offer — religious instruction, some disquieting information has emerged. On the Internet website supported in part by the Alberta ministry responsible for education, teacher access is facilitated through links to a host of resource materials. Under the heading of "Religious Studies," the materials include the following: "We must first believe on Jesus," "Jesus — the Only Way," "Jesus Christ is the Jewish Messiah," "When He finds the unregenerate without Christ, He will not spare them," "[Jesus said] I am the way, the truth, and the life; no man cometh unto the Father, but by me."[77]

As indicated, I don't know to what extent, if at all, such materials are actually used in Alberta's public schools. But I contend nevertheless that the government and its emanations should not be involved in promoting the use of such literature. While it is ethically permissible for the government and the public schools to promote *knowledge about* various religions, it is ethically impermissible for them to promote a *belief in* any particular religion. They have no business promoting such a controversial belief as the deity of Jesus as though it were a matter of incontrovertible fact such as 2+2 = 4 or C-A-T spells *cat*. It is also ethically impermissible for government and its emanations to engage the students in the ritual exercises belonging to any religious faith such as the Lord's Prayer.

Moreover, it is not enough to provide, as the enabling Alberta statute does, for a right of exemption from such instruction and exercises.[78] In the circumstances, such a right is certainly necessary, but it is not sufficient. The conspicuous withdrawal of a child from the classroom for religious reasons is often experienced as an unpleasant disability associated with religious dissent — an experience incompatible with a genuine freedom of religion.

In this connection, consider the experience of a Ba'hai family during the time that religious instruction was part of the Ontario public school curriculum. The parents were unwilling to exempt their ten-year-old daughter from religious classes even though they suspected that certain nightmares she suffered were related to what she had learned there. After the religious teacher warned the class that non-Christians would go to hell, the little girl reportedly dreamt that the devil was chasing her. Notwithstanding this ordeal, the parents refused to exercise their right of exemption because their daughter was even more afraid of being singled out as different by her classmates.[79] Such experiences (there have been many others) revealed the inadequacy of exemption as a remedy for religious dissenters.

All this is very unfair. The youngsters of all religious groups are compelled to attend school. They are not, therefore, "fair game" for such efforts at indoctrination.

A variant of the religious instruction issue arose during the late 1990s in British Columbia. The Surrey school board in that province was faced with a request that it approve, for educational resource use in kindergarten and grade 1, certain books that portrayed families headed by same-sex couples as normal and socially acceptable. The school board's response was to enact a resolution that provided in part as follows: "Therefore be it resolved that all administration, teaching, and counselling staff be informed that resources from gay and lesbian groups ... are not approved for use or redistribution in the Surrey School District."[80]

Instead of affirmatively promoting a particular conception of a Divine Will, the school board here invoked such a theological doctrine to *withhold* material from its classrooms. It appears that, to a great extent, this resolution represented an attempt to appease a large number of ratepayers who claimed the material in question offended their religious sensibilities. Moreover, the vote cast by at least one of the trustees seems to have been influenced by her own theological objections to homosexuality.[81]

The position adopted by the Surrey school board diametrically contravened what should be a guiding principle of the current war on terrorism. *No one's* intuitions about God has any business determining the policies of a public school board. Such boards, of course, properly promote matters of fact. As for values, the role of a public school board is to stimulate reflective inquiry and critical thinking. In addition, such public agencies properly propagate that which enjoys a universal consensus of support in the community, including such values as courtesy, kindness, honesty, loyalty, and diligence. It is certainly appropriate for public school boards to identify such values as "good." But it is inappropriate for public school authorities to teach, as a fact, that such values derive their validity from God, Jesus, Allah, or dialectical materialism.

There is no suggestion that the impugned books in this controversy, in any way, attempted to promote homosexuality as virtuous, enjoyable, or desirable. Apparently, however, these books did endeavour to impart to the students that their communities contained a number of families headed by same-sex couples that provided a loving atmosphere in which children could grow up. That, of course, was presumably a fact. The books also strove to create a social climate in which people from same-sex families could be accepted and respected. This value, as reflected in the Charter and many human-rights statutes, enjoys a consensus of support in Canada. Exactly what public school boards should be promoting!

While the Supreme Court of Canada ultimately vitiated this Surrey school board resolution, we cannot afford to be sanguine about what comparable controversies lie in store for us. We know there is a strong propensity to resolve social problems on the basis of a presumed Divine Will. It is not good enough to rely on the courts to straighten us out. Aggrieved persons won't always have the resources and stamina for the waging of a court fight. All of us must learn to think more clearly about these kinds of issues. Just as the functionaries of al-Qaeda are determined to inflict their theology on everyone, everywhere, *we* must be no less determined to keep such theology in its proper place.

◆

Just as it is important to ensure that no one's theology is allowed to prevail over the populace, no one's theology should be protected from the criticisms of the populace. Indeed, in many ways, this concept is the essence of freedom of expression and of religion in a viable democracy. While such freedoms continue to enjoy general respect in our society, they are being seriously challenged in at least one vital sector. Paradoxically, that sector is one that virtually defines itself in terms of such freedoms — the university.

Historically, our universities have been key bastions of intellectual ferment. These institutions have not only permitted, but they have also encouraged open and vigorous debate about all kinds of ideas — political, philosophical, ideological, and religious. Unfortunately, Canadian universities have sustained a significant erosion of this vital role. To the extent that such erosion is allowed to continue, our society stands to lose a key component of its intellectual nourishment. No democracy can long retain its viability in a state of such deprivation.

A case history will serve to illustrate this phenomenon. In the late winter or early spring of 2001 — a few months before 9/11

157

— a disciplinary investigation was launched against a student at Toronto's Osgoode Hall Law School because of an article he had published in his school's newspaper.[82] The student's article accused the Islamic religion of being "oppressive, backwards, and brutal ... an affront to basic human dignity." It also charged that Islam is "a hybrid ... of the worst elements of communism and fascism coexisting in a monstrous symbiosis."[83]

The cause of the investigation was a complaint that another student had filed alleging the article violated a campus regulation prohibiting "harassment or discrimination in contravention of the principles articulated in the Ontario Human Rights Code."[84] Such regulations have been adopted at many universities across Canada. The goal, of course, is a worthy one. As expressed by the then dean of the law school, the idea is to ensure that "students are able to study ... in an atmosphere" where they don't have to "endure attacks on their dignity and self-worth based on their creed, race, colour" or other similar grounds.[85]

No one whose enlightenment exceeds that of a Neanderthal could possibly quarrel with so noble an objective. The problem, however, is not the goal; it is the means. In order to achieve its worthy objective, the regulation infringes on the heart of university life: freedom of expression. This freedom means that religious beliefs, no less than philosophical theories and political doctrines, must be fair game for the challenges and criticisms of university students. Whether the targeted doctrines stem from Christianity, Judaism, Islam, conservatism, liberalism, socialism, capitalism, or Marxism, they should enjoy no immunity from the critical scrutiny of the campus community.

During the course of the debates that led to the adoption of these anti-harassment regulations, it was often argued that freedom of expression at the university level need not include taunting, hectoring, and pestering. According to the advocates of these restrictions on speech, no *legitimate* expression is imperilled by banning such nuisance behaviour. But even if this argument were accepted, it had nothing to do with the circumstances of this case. The author of the impugned article was not taunting, hectoring, or pestering. He was simply expressing an opinion. This is what intellectual freedom at a university is supposed to be about. The fact that the opinion he expressed was hostile to the Muslim faith should make no difference to his right to express it.

Admittedly, a number of the statements in the impugned article are, at the very least, unpleasant. Nor would there be any doubt that numbers of Muslims and even non-Muslims would be offended by them. But even if it were assumed, as the Osgoode Hall dean reportedly commented, that "the article … made some unjustified criticisms of the Islamic belief system,"[86] the question remains: should anyone have to face a disciplinary investigation and perhaps even an expulsion for having written such a piece in a university publication?

The defenders of these restrictions on speech have argued that there is no need for campus discussion to be so vitriolic. But religious, philosophical, and political disputes often engage the deepest passions; it would be unacceptably artificial to insist that such passions be removed from campus controversies. While the university must not tolerate acts or threats of physical violence, it must be open to the most biting of criticisms. Even though civility in discourse would be desirable, the question is whether incivility should be permissible. Why should *university* discussion be so uniquely subject to a legal obligation that it be expressed in terms of endearment, tones of affection, or according to the canons of Emily Post?

To whatever extent members of the campus community express "unjustified criticisms" of any belief or ideology, they should receive not disciplinary coercion, but critical discussion. In this regard, I recall a conversation I had with an American university dean a few years ago. He pointed out how he had joined a student picket line in protest against a visiting speaker who was expressing particularly bigoted views. He said that he was happy to register his disapproval of the speaker but was adamantly opposed to the censorship of his views.

This kind of approach is one that Canadian universities would do well to emulate. To whatever extent faculty members

believe that student debates may unfairly malign a religious doctrine, such professors should join the discussion so that the entire
campus community can benefit from their expertise. In view of
the increased vulnerability of Muslim students since 9/11, faculty
involvement of this sort would be especially desirable when it is
believed that Islam has been unfairly attacked. It is crucial, however, to observe the distinction between defending an ideology
and muzzling its critics.

As indicated by the Osgoode Hall case and a number of others across Canada, this is a distinction that universities may have
to learn all over again.

✦

In some situations, the excessive promotion of religion has taken
yet another form. During the past several years, there have been
growing pressures in Canada for governments to provide religious
day schools with significant amounts of public tax money.[87] The
claim for this is bolstered by the fact that, in a number of jurisdic-
tions, there is a constitutional requirement to provide such funding for the Roman Catholic separate schools. But public support
for the Catholic schools is an inheritance from bargains that were
made in a much earlier era. In some cases, such bargains are so old
and so basic that they helped to make possible Confederation in
Canada.[88] In any event, these benefits for the Catholic schools are
generally not attributable to any contemporary initiatives.

Government funding of religious schools beyond what is
already constitutionally required would mean that the schools from
virtually *all* religions would be entitled to comparable treatment.
To whatever extent this process continued and increased, further
proliferation would be encouraged. At some point even mainstream
Protestants could well be enticed to open their own schools. In consequence, public school enrolments could dwindle dramatically.

A country in which so many, perhaps most, youngsters attend-
ed separate religious schools would likely be a much different place
from what it is today. The ordeals of the twentieth century, and

thus far the twenty-first century, have demonstrated the fragility of inter-religious and inter-ethnic co-existence. In so many ways, inter-group tension appears to be endemic to the human condition. Wise social policy requires that we do all we can to address our xenophobic and parochial propensities.

According to a review of the social science literature, "in all the surveys in all communities and for all groups, majority and minorities, the greater the frequency of interaction, the lower the prevalence of ethnic prejudice."[89] For all their faults, therefore, the common public schools provide us with a unique opportunity to promote inter-group cooperation and respect. When youngsters of all racial, religious, and ethnic backgrounds work together in the classroom, play together in the school yard, and eat together in the cafeteria, they are enabled to develop the habits of inter-group rapport that can last a lifetime.

The public schools can also serve as an instrument to advance democratic values among those who have come to this country from authoritarian cultures. This is not to predict, of course, that such good things necessarily will result. It is simply to contend that, as between stratification and integration, the latter provides at least significantly more opportunity. On this basis, I believe governments in Canada should reverse the process in which public money is extended to religious schools. The proliferation of such assistance means more religious segregation in our educational institutions. Such a policy can weaken the ability of the democracies to wage the ideological component of our conflict against terrorism.

Inadequate Protection of Religion

While we are doing too much to promote religious belief, we are not doing enough to *protect* it. In order to compete for the hearts and minds of people around the world, our society must be a showcase of respect for diversity. Unfortunately, there are situations in which governments in Canada have adopted measures affirmatively restricting expressions of religious belief.

In this connection, consider the "bubble zone" legislation in British Columbia. It empowers the government to forbid "any act of disapproval ... with respect to ... abortion services, by any means, including ... graphic, verbal or written ..." within fifty metres of certain abortion clinics.[90] In short, anti-abortionists may be prevented from expressing their disapproval of abortion within half a football field of such clinics.

It is one thing to protect doctors and patients from physical obstruction; it is another thing entirely to immunize them from social disapproval. Nor is it any answer to say, as some have, that the anti-abortion protesters can always express their views somewhere else. That reminds me of a statement I made a number of years ago in another context: "In Canada, we don't ban demonstrations, we reroute them."

As an example of how excessive these B.C. restrictions might be, certain clinic staff members demanded that the police arrest some protesters for merely *praying* within a prohibited zone.[91] Admittedly, where health facilities are concerned, there is a case for picketing restrictions that would not be justified in other situations. Even so, there is no excuse for the *magnitude* of restrictions that were made possible in British Columbia. Freedom of religious expression — even freedom of expression itself — sustained an unwarranted hit in that province.

At the time of this writing, the Saskatchewan Human Rights Commission is pursuing a self-styled Christian fundamentalist who placed an advertisement in one of that province's major newspapers. The advertisement showed a diagonal line drawn through the image of two men holding hands; the image was accompanied by Biblical citations deeply critical of homosexual practices.[92]

I have no hesitation in condemning the advertisement as repugnant and even acknowledging that, if the newspaper had rejected it, I would not likely have protested. But *illegality* is another story.

The Saskatchewan commission argued that banning the advertisement would interfere only minimally with the fundamentalist's freedom of religious expression. According to the commission, he was still free to read his Bible, donate money, talk to his fellow believers, and distribute Bibles.[93] But in order to have their views even considered, activists must often employ attention-getting measures. To confine proselytizers to polite discussion is — to paraphrase a famous British author — to replace freedom of communication with freedom of soliloquy.

In the early part of the twenty-first century, the Ontario Human Rights Commission launched proceedings against a printer who refused to print the stationery of a gay and lesbian organization.[94] As a "born-again Christian," the printer insisted that he conscientiously objected to this job. In the opinion of the board of inquiry established by the commission to hear the complaint against the printer, his "reason for refusing to provide the printing services was the sexual orientation of either the members of the [organization], or the sexual orientation of the community it serves."[95] Significantly, however, the board of inquiry also concluded that if the gay complainant had "sought personal printing services for a purpose unrelated to the [organization] he would have received the service." In short, the impugned proprietor would have printed the stationery of a gay dentist. Yet the board held that the printer had violated the Human Rights Code.

While I share the disdain of the commission and the board of inquiry for this printer's views about homosexuality, I believe that his position should have been defended. While those who operate businesses in the public market should be required to serve gay persons, they should not be comparably obliged to serve gay *causes*. It is clear from the quoted remarks that the human-rights enforcement authorities in Ontario did not buy this distinction.

Consider the implications. While it is incontestable that a black printer could not lawfully discriminate against white persons, the thrust of this decision might equally hold that such a printer could not refuse service to the Ku Klux Klan. Similarly, a gay printer could not refuse to serve an anti-gay, religious fundamentalist cause. While the Ontario Divisional Court did somewhat alter the judgment of the board of inquiry, I am concerned nevertheless about the intellectual orientation of those entrusted to enforce our human-rights laws. A viable freedom of conscience requires more sophisticated distinctions than they were disposed to make.

As a result of policies adopted by a municipality in the province of Quebec, the Jehovah's Witnesses became effectively precluded from building a temple there to practise their faith. Upon finding themselves unable to obtain a landowner who would make the requisite property available to them within the boundaries of the appropriate zone, the Witnesses attempted to buy land located in a commercial zone. In order to validate the transaction, they requested the municipality to approve a zoning change. In its final decision on the matter, the municipality expressed itself in part as follows: "After deliberating, the municipality of Lafontaine has decided not to act on your applications. The ... council is not required to provide any justification; consequently, we do not intend to give the grounds for the council's decision."[96]

Inevitably, such high-handed treatment generates suspicions of religious discrimination. This is hardly the kind of behaviour likely to impress the world with Canada's sense of fairness. The demands of our contemporary situation require a more hospitable response to religious minorities than was forthcoming from this Quebec municipality. Even though the Supreme Court of Canada ultimately reversed this decision, there is little basis for consolation. Court challenges are demanding, expensive and, therefore, rare. Social and political mores must change.

Just as it is necessary for us to find and thwart the terrorists in our midst, it is also necessary that we improve our perspective as regards the promotion and protection of religious belief. Our democratic ideology must not be neglected.

A Concluding Word

As indicated at the outset, my concern has been to identify ethical fallacies in the way Canada's response to terrorism has been analyzed. For these purposes, the conclusions that are reached take a back seat to the methods that are used.

That is why I focused so much on the misconceived criteria employed by the commentators on American policy in Iraq. The object of the exercise was not to evaluate the merits of the war; it was to assess the quality of the debate about the war. The idea was to identify the major fallacies that appeared to be influencing the debate. My primary interest here is to counsel against making these kinds of analytical mistakes the next time we face issues or crises in the war against terrorism.

Similarly, even if some of the questions I raised about Canada's anti-terror laws were to be satisfactorily answered, that would not mean the questions were not worth raising. Again what I am seeking to ensure is that we are always asking the right questions.

On the international front, the critical factor is that much of the arena is a jungle in which the rule of law cannot operate. Thus, for the sake of a rule of law that does not exist, the democracies should not fetter their ability to act. In the dangerous jungle out there, the most important task for the democracies is to ensure that their precious institutions can survive in viable condition. It is not sensible, therefore, that free societies seek permission from unfree societies in order to defend any of their vital values. Thus, insistence on deference to the United Nations emerged as a key fallacy.

Ethically, democracies must have the kind of latitude we would not hesitate to withhold from dictatorships. Therefore, it is fallacious to insist on single standards that apply to both kinds of regimes equally. The exercise of trying to preserve a dictatorship safeguards the power to abuse. The exercise of trying to preserve a democracy promotes the avoidance of abuse. It is wrong then to treat them equally. Hence, the fallacy that I call "equivalence mongering."

None of the above suggests that even in the international jungle, the democracies are ethically entitled to do whatever they please. Even though they need not be constrained by the requirements of an inoperable rule of law, they must nevertheless attempt to limit the injuries they might cause. Thus, in a military situation they must do everything they reasonably can to avoid civilian casualties.

At home, however, the rule of law can, and usually does, operate. In view of its centrality to the dignified treatment of human beings, the democracies have a special ethical obligation to protect it. That is the reason I have attempted to identify so many fallacies in the way the government of Canada (and even of the United States) has sought to bypass the fundamental safeguards of the democratic system.

Hence the difficulty I have with the post-9/11 power to list people as terrorist entities and to require that the rest of us avoid certain dealings with them — all without a prior hearing before an independent tribunal. In short, a unilateral act on the part of the government can transform a person into a virtual pariah. The government pushed this measure without properly explaining why less repressive measures could not adequately achieve its legitimate objectives.

The same thing happened with a number of the government's other post-9/11 measures, including the requirement that individuals become informers and provide investigative assistance, the increased powers to wiretap and detain, the ability to withdraw public processes from public scrutiny, the expanded anti-hate provisions, and the amount of police control over access to the areas near international conferences. The government of Canada has yet to provide the people of Canada with an adequate demonstration of the need for these additional departures from traditional freedoms.

Acknowledging, as we must, that situations arise when it may be truly necessary to encroach on our fundamental freedoms, we should insist nevertheless that such encroachments do not exceed what the situation reasonably requires. This requirement is the principle of "minimal impairment."

In this regard, as well, Canada's post-9/11 behaviour is laden with fallacies. Consider the prohibition against providing assistance to ideologically motivated violence that is designed to coerce governments anywhere in the world. This prohibition is formulated in such broad terms that it could now be a crime for Canadians to donate money to an armed indigenous insurrection against the governments of China, Iran, or North Korea. It is hard, of course, to criticize a ban on helping anti-democratic uprisings that deliberately target innocent civilians for serious violence. But why in the world should such a prohibition be extended any farther than that? After all, certain repressive dictatorships are not likely to be removed without some amount of violence.

That is what happens when the principle of minimal impairment is not respected. We wind up criminalizing behaviour that is altogether legitimate, even desirable. I think it is also fair to challenge the government of Canada to demonstrate why such broad measures are needed in the fight against terrorism. Indeed, in the case of the above example, over-inclusive prohibitions are capable of undermining even *anti*-terror efforts.

If I had to summarize the essence of the ethical fallacies that have hitherto bedevilled Canada's war against terrorism, I would do so in the following way. Internationally, key fallacies stem from an undue respect for a rule of law that does not exist. Domestically, key fallacies stem from an undue neglect of a rule of law that does exist.

There is every reason to believe that the fight against terrorism will be long and hard. There are no quick fixes or easy panaceas. If democracy is to survive, as it must, we will have to steel ourselves for the struggle.

If any further incentive is indicated, we need only contemplate what will happen if we *don't* do what the struggle requires. On the one hand, there is the spectre of ultimate terrorist victory with countries around the world unwillingly succumbing to the most extreme version of Islamic law with its torture chambers, stoning of adulterous adolescents, and mutilation of felons. On the other hand, there is the spectre of internal repression such as North America experienced with the 1940s incarceration of innocent Japanese people and the 1950s persecution of innocent left-wingers.

Abroad we must be ready for military action — preemptively if necessary — with or without United Nations authorization. At home we must strive to minimize encroachments on fundamental freedoms, with special care to avoid the persecution and harassment of Arabs and Muslims, the overwhelming number of whom are innocent of wrongdoing. A good place to start is to identify the indiscriminate fallacies that have impeded us so far. To be sure, such identification will not be sufficient, but without doubt it is necessary.

Notes

A Beginning Word

1. David Bamber, *Daily Telegraph* (United Kingdom), November 11, 2001.
2. Transcript of an interview with John Miller of *ABC News*, May 1998. See *www.pbs.org/wgbh/pages/frontline/shows/bin-laden/who/interview.html*.
3. *Ibid.*
4. David Bamber, *Daily Telegraph*.
5. John Miller, "Greetings, America — My Name Is Osama Bin Laden," *Esquire*, Vol. 131, No. 2 (February 1999).
6. "Interview: Conversation Terror (Interview with Osama Bin Laden)," *Time*, January 11, 1999.
7. Lisa Beyer, "The Most Wanted Man in the World," *Time*, September 24, 2001.
8. From Osama bin Laden's taped remarks aired on al-Jazeera on Sunday, October 7, 2001, and reported by *USA Today*.
9. Daniel Pipes, "We're Going to Conquer America," *New York Post*, November 12, 2001.
10. Yossef Bodansky, *Bin Laden: The Man Who Declared War on America* (Rocklin, CA: Forum Press, 2001).
11. Transcript of an interview with John Miller of *ABC News*.
12. Osama bin Laden's November 2002 "Letter to the American People" as reported in the *Observer* (United Kingdom) on November 24, 2002.
13. Transcript of an interview with John Miller of *ABC News*.
14. David Bamber, *Daily Telegraph*.
15. Transcript of an interview with Sheila MacVicar of *ABC News*, January 14, 1999.
16. "Interview: Conversation Terror (Interview with Osama Bin Laden)."
17. "Declaration of War Against the Americans Occupying the Land of the Two Holy Places," issued by Osama Bin Laden on

August 23, 1996. See "Bin Laden's Fatwah" at *www.pbs.org/newshour/terrorism/international/fatwa_1996.html.*

18. "Fatwah Urging Jihad Against Americans," published in *Al-Quds al-'Arabi* on February 23, 1998.

19. "Interview: Conversation Terror (Interview with Osama Bin Laden)."

20. Interview with Osama bin Laden by CNN's Peter Arnett in eastern Afghanistan in late March 1997.

21. Bodansky, *Bin Laden: The Man Who Declared War on America.*

22. Paul Berman, *Terror and Liberalism* (New York: W.W. Norton, 2003).

Part I: Abroad

Chapter 1: In General

1. Jerry Falwell made the remarks on the television program *The 700 Club* just after the attacks, as widely reported in the news media, including CNN. See *http://archives.cnn.com/2001/US/09/14/Falwell.apology.*

2. Noam Chomsky, "Drain the Swamp and There Will Be No More Mosquitoes," *The Guardian*, September 9, 2002.

3. Jim Selby, Alberta Federation of Labour, *Evidence,* Meeting No. 82, May 9, 2002.

4. Haroon Siddiqui, "Tutu Berates Bellicose Bush," *Toronto Star*, September 26, 2002.

5. William Dalrymple, "A Largely Bourgeois Endeavour: Al-Qaida-Style Terrorists Are Not the Type Who Seek Out Madrasas," *The Guardian* (United Kingdom), July 20, 2005.

6. "Poverty, Political Freedom, and the Roots of Terror" — "Associate Professor of Public Policy Alberto Abadie examined data on terrorism and variables such as wealth, political freedom, geography, and ethnic fractionalization for nations that have been targets of terrorist attacks. Abadie, whose

work was published in the Kennedy School's Faculty Research Working Paper Series, included both acts of international and domestic terrorism in his analysis." From "Freedom Squelches Terrorist Violence," *Harvard University Gazette*, November 4, 2004. Note also Guy Giorno's article in the *Toronto Star* on September 22, 2002, citing "Princeton Professor Alan Krueger and Czech scholar Jitka Maleckova [who] surveyed the available evidence and concluded that, if anything, the connection is between terrorism and higher socio-economic status."

7. Linda McQuaig, "Terror Attacks Are Response to Military Actions," *Toronto Star*, July 31, 2005.

8. *Ibid.*

9. This quote is cited by Linda McQuaig from Robert Pape, "a political scientist at the University of Chicago and director of the Chicago Project on Suicide Terrorism," in "Terror Attacks Are Response to Military Actions," *Toronto Star*, July 31, 2005.

10. Osama bin Laden's November 2002 "Letter to the American People."

11. *Ibid.*

12. Berman, *Terror and Liberalism*, 91.

13. Lawrence Wright, "The Terror Web," *The New Yorker*, August 2, 2004.

14. Jonathan Freedland, "It's Not Only About Iraq," *The Guardian*, July 20, 2005.

15. Right Reverend Dr. Marion Pardy, letter to the *National Post*, April 5, 2002.

16. Rick Salutin, *Globe and Mail*, exchange with Keith Landy, May 25, 2002.

17. A letter to Anglicans from Primate Peers, April 5, 2002.

18. *Ibid.*

19. Rick Salutin, "Bush: Dumb by Choice," *Globe and Mail*, May 24, 2002.

20. Haroon Siddiqui, "Tutu: No Security Without Justice," *Toronto Star*, July 15, 2004.

21. Verified on December 28, 2005, by Nancy Knickerbocker, director of media relations with the B.C. Teachers' Federation.

22. From the text of a speech to the New Democratic Party's national council meeting, October 13, 2001.

23. Hansard, October 15, 2001.

24. Michael Mandel, "Say What You Want, but This War Is Illegal," *Globe and Mail*, October 9, 2001.

25. Tim Harper, "Graham Insists on Israeli Pullback," *Toronto Star*, April 3, 2002.

26. *Toronto Star*, "Timely Nobel Message," October 12, 2002.

27. Haroon Siddiqui, "World Still Wary of Bush War Case," *Toronto Star*, October 10, 2002.

28. James Travers, *Toronto Star*, September 19, 2002.

29. Richard Gwyn, *Toronto Star*, September 15, 2002.

30. Lloyd Axworthy, "Beware the Fever of War," *Globe and Mail*, October 8, 2002.

31. David Ljunggren, "U.S. Has No Right to Invade Iraq, Canada Says," Reuters, October 2, 2002.

32. Kofi Annan, "Address to the General Assembly of the United Nations," September 12, 2002.

33. As regards France, see Evelyn Irtani, "Hussein's Government Signs Lucrative Contracts, Especially with Nations That Oppose the U.S. Led Effort to Oust the Regime," *Los Angeles Times*, November 11, 2002; as regards Russia, see Ariel Cohen's testimony to the U.S House of Representatives International Relations Committee, February 26, 2003, in a presentation entitled, "Russia and the Axis of Evil: Money, Ambition and U.S. Interests."

34. Ed Morgan, *National Post*, October 24, 2002.

35. John Polanyi, "World at the Crossroads: Law or War? — Inaugural Lecture in Honour of Acharya Sushil Kumar," January 17, 2003.

36. Telford Taylor, *Munich: The Price of Peace* (New York: Doubleday, 1979), 998–1000; William L. Shirer, *20th Century Journey. A Memoir of the Life and the Times: Vol. II:*

The Nightmare Years, 1930–1940 (Boston: Little Brown, 1984), 250.

37. Haroon Siddiqui, *Toronto Star*, October 2, 2002.
38. Richard Gwyn, *Toronto Star*, September 22, 2002.
39. James Travers, *Toronto Star*, September 19, 2002.
40. Kimon Valaskakis, *Globe and Mail*, September 17, 2002.
41. Richard Gwyn, *Toronto Star*, September 4, 2002.
42. Advertisement published September 19, 2002, in the *New York Times*.
43. Graciously confirmed by Janice Stein via email, February 7, 2006.
44. Haroon Siddiqui, *Toronto Star*, October 6, 2002.
45. George W. Bush's "National Security Strategy 2002," promulgating the so-called "Bush Doctrine," as reported in Joshua Muravchik, "The Bush Manifesto," *Commentary*, Vol. 114, No. 5 (December 2002).
46. Linda McQuaig, *Toronto Star*, September 29, 2002.
47. Thomas Walkom, *Toronto Star*, September 10, 2002.
48. Michael Mandel, *Globe and Mail*, October 9, 2001.
49. Amnesty International press release, "Israel Shows Reckless Disregard for Human Life," issued August 1, 2002.
50. *Ibid.*
51. Ralph Peters, *Wall Street Journal*, July 25, 2002.
52. *Ibid.*
53. Rick Salutin, *Globe and Mail*, April 5, 2002.
54. *Ibid.*
55. Haroon Siddiqui, *Toronto Star*, March 31, 2002.
56. Charles Krauthammer, *National Post*, August 8, 2003.
57. *Ibid.*
58. Henry Seigman, *International Herald Tribune*, January 27, 2005.
59. *Beit Sourik Village Council v. the Government of Israel*, HCJ 2056/04, June 30, 2004; "Israel's Security Fence Doesn't Trump Justice," editorial, *Globe and Mail*, July 2, 2004.
60. "I call on the Palestinian people to elect new leaders, leaders not compromised by terror. I call upon them to build a

practicing democracy based on tolerance and liberty." —
George W. Bush, press conference, June 24, 2002. See
www.whitehouse.gov.

61. Rick Salutin, *Globe and Mail,* June 28, 2002.

62. *Ibid.*

Chapter 2: On Iraq

1. Richard Gwyn, *Toronto Star,* December 22, 2002.

2. *Ibid.*

3. See, for example, UNMOVIC 12th Quarterly Report to
   the Security Council, "Unresolved Disarmament Issues:
   Iraq's Proscribed Weapons Programmes" (March 6, 2003),
   67, 76, 77.

4. Letter dated April 6, 1991, from the minister of foreign
   affairs of Iraq to the United Nations Security Council.

5. United Nations Security Council Resolution 687 (April 3,
   1991), (S/RES/687).

6. United Nations Security Council Resolution 1441
   (November 8, 2002), (S/RES/1441).

7. Hans Blix, *Notes for Briefing the Security Council,* January 9,
   2003.

8. *Ibid.*

9. Richard Butler, remarks to the Seventh Carnegie
   International Non-Proliferation Conference, Washington,
   D.C., January 11 and 12, 1999, found at *www.ceip.org/pro-
   grams/npp/butler99.htm*; transcript of a PBS *Frontline* interview with Richard Butler in 1999 (see PBS's *Frontline* website at *www.pbs.org/wgbh/pages/frontline*); Joseph Cirincone et
   al., "WMD in Iraq: Evidence and Implications," Carnegie
   Endowment for International Peace's website
   (*www.carnegieendowment.org*), January 7, 2004, 82; Charles
   Duelfer, "Comprehensive Report of the Special Advisor to
   the Director of Central Intelligence on Iraq's WMD," Vol.
   1, Central Intelligence Agency's website (*www.cia.gov*),
   September 30, 2004, 8.

10. See Norman Podhoretz, "Who Is Lying About Iraq?" *Commentary*, December 2005.

11. Senator Edward Kennedy, "Eliminating the Threat: The Right Course of Action for Disarming Iraq, Combating Terrorism, Protecting the Homeland, and Stabilizing the Middle East," speech delivered at Johns Hopkins University, September 27, 2002.

12. "Kennedy Says Iraq War Case a 'Fraud,'" *New York Times*, September 18, 2003.

13. Allan Thompson, "Canadians Balk at Iraq War," *Toronto Star*, September 9, 2002.

14. Tim Harper, "Poll: Canadians Sour on U.S.," *Toronto Star*, December 7, 2002.

15. Haroon Siddiqui, *Toronto Star*, September 26, 2002.

16. Haroon Siddiqui, *Toronto Star*, October 10, 2002.

17. Interview with Nelson Mandela in *Newsweek*, September 10, 2002.

18. Richard Gwyn, *Toronto Star*, October 20, 2002.

19. Linda McQuaig, *Toronto Star*, September 15, 2002.

20. Richard Gwyn, *Toronto Star*, September 18, 2002.

21. Richard Gwyn, *Toronto Star*, September 4, 2002.

22. Linda McQuaig; *Toronto Star*, February 9, 2003.

23. See, for example, UNMOVIC 12th Quarterly Report to the Security Council, "Unresolved Disarmament Issues: Iraq's Proscribed Weapons Programmes" (March 6, 2003), 124.

24. Warren Allmand, Ed Broadbent, and Flora MacDonald, *Globe and Mail*, February 15, 2003.

25. Charles Krauthammer, *Washington Post*, January 10, 2003.

26. See Faye Bowers, "Driving Forces in War-Wary Nations: The Stances of France, Germany, Russia and China are Colored by Economic and National Interests," *Christian Science Monitor*, February 23, 2003.

27. Rick Salutin, *Globe and Mail*, February 7, 2003.

28. Stephen J. Hedges and Douglas Holt, "North Korea No Easy Win, Analysts Say," *Chicago Tribune*, February 9, 2003.

29. Paul Cellucci's remarks were reported by Andrew Coyne, *National Post*, March 26, 2003.
30. Margaret Wente, *Globe and Mail*, March 27, 2003.
31. *Ibid.*
32. Rick Anderson, *Toronto Star*, July 13, 2003.
33. "President Bush Discusses Iraq Report," White House press release, October 7, 2004.
34. *Ibid.*
35. Norman Podhoretz, *Commentary*, September 2004.
36. George W. Bush's address to the American Enterprise Institute, February, 2003. See *www.whitehouse.gov/news/releases/2003/02/print/20030226-11.html*.
37. Norman Spector, *Globe and Mail*, July 4, 2003.
38. Arnon Regular, *Ha'aretz*, June 23, 2003.
39. Mark MacKinnon, "Power Outages Generating Anger in Iraq," *Globe and Mail*, December 20, 2003. See also note 52 in this chapter.
40. James Risen, "Secrets of History: The CIA in Iran — A Special Report: How a Plot Convulsed Iran in '53 (and in '79)," *New York Times*, April 16, 2000. See also Mark J. Gasiorowski and Malcolm Byrne, eds., *Mohammad Mosaddeq and the 1953 Coup in Iran* (Syracuse, NY: Syracuse University Press, 2004).
41. On Dr. Phan Quang Dan, see Chester A. Bain, *Vietnam: The Roots of Conflict* (Englewood Cliffs, NJ: Prentice Hall, 1967), 99; on Thich Tri Quang, see, for example, "The Buddhist Revolt in Vietnam," *Dissent*, Vol. 13, No. 3 (May-June 1966), 227.
42. See Theodore Draper, *Castro's Revolution: Myths and Realities* (Boulder, CO.: Frederick A. Praeger, 1962), 59–113.
43. "CIA Is Accused by Bitter Rebels," *New York Times*, April 22, 1961; "Underground Force Quits Revolutionary Group to Protest CIA Action," *New York Times*, May 24, 1961; Wayne Smith, *The Closest of Enemies* (New York: W.W. Norton, 1987), 71–72.
44. *Ibid.*

45. Draper, *Castro's Revolution*, 25–26 and 66–67.
46. Salvador E. Gomez, "The U.S. Invasion of the Dominican Republic: 1965," *Sincronia* (Spring 1997).
47. *Ibid.*
48. Shirley Christian, *Nicaragua: Revolution in the Family* (New York: Random House, 1985).
49. *Ibid.*
50. "North's Liaison Man Heard Plot Devised to Kill Contra Leader," *Globe and Mail*, January 7, 1987.
51. Speech by President George W. Bush delivered on June 24, 2002.
52. Michael Schwartz, "How the Bush Administration Dismantled Iraq," *TomDispatch.com* (Nation Institute On-Line), available at *www.tomdispatch.com/index.mhtml?pid=84463*.
53. For an overview account of the scandal, see, for example, Bradley Graham, "A Failure in Leadership, All the Way Up the Ranks," *Washington Post*, August 24, 2004. See also Mark Danner, *Torture and Truth: America, Abu Ghraib, and the War on Terror* (New York: New York Review Books, 2004).
54. Naomi Klein, "Let's Put Teeth in Our Protest," *Globe and Mail*, November 30, 2004.
55. *Ibid.*
56. Ali Akbar Dareini, "Iran's President Calls Holocaust a 'Myth,'" *Globe and Mail*, December 14, 2005.

Part II: At Home

Chapter 1: In General

1. Verified by Anne McLellan over the telephone, May 8, 2006.
2. David Schneiderman, "Terrorism and the Risk Society," in R.J. Daniels, P. Macklem, and K. Roach, eds., *The Security of Freedom: Essays on Canada's Anti-Terrorism Bill* (Toronto: University of Toronto Press, 2001).

3. Gary Trotter, "The Anti-Terrorism Bill and Preventative Restraints on Liberty," in Daniels, Macklem, and Roach, *The Security of Freedom.*

4. Don Stuart, "The Dangers of Quick Fix Legislation in the Criminal Law: The Anti-Terrorism Bill C-36 Should Be Withdrawn," in Daniels, Macklem, and Roach, *The Security of Freedom.*

5. Verified by Anne McLellan over the telephone, May 8, 2006.

6. *Ibid.*

7. Commission of Inquiry Concerning Certain Activities of the RCMP (McDonald Commission), *Freedom and Security Under the Law*, Second Report, Vol. 1 (Ottawa: Supply and Services, 1981), 203–09.

8. On November 26, 2001, New Democratic Party MP Joe Comartin said the following in the House of Commons, as reported in Hansard (37th Parliament, 1st Session, No. 118): "It is reported from the archives that with regard to Mr. Lewis the reason they were investigating him, according to one of the intelligence officers ... was that he was 'disposed to criticism of the existing political structure.'" See also Allen L. Kagedan, "What History Teaches: The Case of David Lewis," published by the Canadian Intelligence Resource Centre, September 28, 2002. According to this paper, "the RCMP held a file on David Lewis from 1931 to 1984, three years after his death." This information is supported by Jim Bronskill, "Committed Socialist David Lewis Was Under Police Scrutiny for More Than 50 Years," *Ottawa Citizen*, November 23, 2001.

9. *Ibid.*

Chapter 2: Expanding the Offences

1. Criminal Code s. 83.01 (1)(b)(ii)(E).

2. Criminal Code s. 83.01 (1)(b)(i)(A).

3. Criminal Code s. 83.01 (1)(b)(ii)(C): "causes a serious risk to the health or safety of the public or any segment of the public."

4. Criminal Code s. 83.01 (1)(b)(ii)(E): "other than as a result of advocacy, protest, dissent or stoppage of work that is not intended to result in the conduct or harm referred to in any of clauses (A) to (C)."
5. Criminal Code s. 83.01 (1)(b)(ii)(E).
6. Glanville Williams, *The Criminal Law: The General Part* (London: Stevens & Sons, 1953), 705–06.
7. Criminal Code s. 83.2: "Every one who commits an indictable offence under this or any other Act of Parliament for the benefit of, at the direction of or in association with a terrorist group is guilty of an indictable offence and liable to imprisonment for life."
8. "Ukrainian Protesters Keep Up Pressure," *Globe and Mail*, November 23, 2004.
9. Viktor Yushchenko's speech to protestors as reported by Paul Quinn-Judge and Yuri Zarakhovich in "The Orange Revolution," *Time*, December 6, 2004.
10. Anne McLellan, testimony before the House of Commons Standing Committee on Justice and Human Rights, October 18, 2001.
11. Protocol Additional to the Geneva Conventions of 12 August 1949, and Relating to the Protection of Victims of International Armed Conflicts ("Protocol I"), adopted on June 8, 1977, by the Diplomatic Conference on the Reaffirmation and Development of International Humanitarian Law Applicable in Armed Conflicts, Article 1, Paragraph 4.
12. Ed Morgan, testimony before the House of Commons Standing Committee on Justice and Human Rights, November 6, 2001.
13. Canadian Civil Liberties Association submissions to the House of Commons Subcommittee on Public Safety and National Security, *Re: Review of the Anti-Terrorism Act*, September 20, 2005, 8–9.
14. McLellan, testimony before the House of Commons Standing Committee on Justice and Human Rights, October 18, 2001.

15. Criminal Code s. 83.08(1)(a).
16. Criminal Code s. 83.1(1).

Chapter 3: The Ostracizing of Terror Suspects

1. Anne McLellan, testimony before the Special Committee on the Subject Matter of Bill C-36, October 22, 2001.
2. Criminal Code s. 83.05(1).
3. Allan Thompson, *Toronto Star*, November 8, 2001.
4. *Ibid.*
5. Anne McLellan, testimony before the House of Commons Standing Committee on Justice and Human Rights, October 18, 2001.
6. On Hezbollah, see Allan Thompson, "Hezbollah Ban in Works, Caplan Says," *Toronto Star*, November 30, 2002; on the Tamil Tigers, see Stewart Bell, "Tamil Tigers Outlawed: Group Added to Canada's Terror List," *National Post*, April 8, 2006.
7. Editorial, *National Post*, December 22, 2001.
8. Proceedings of the Special Senate Committee on the Subject Matter of Bill C-36, Issue 1 — Evidence, October 22, 2001 (afternoon sitting).
9. *Ibid.*
10. *Ibid.*
11. Note that the seventy-two-hours number is a product of deductive reasoning from the legislation by combining the following: Criminal Code s. 83.3(6)(b) — "a person detained in custody shall be taken before a provincial court judge ... [and] if a provincial court judge is not available within a period of twenty-four hours after the person has been arrested, the person shall be taken before a provincial court judge as soon as possible"; and Criminal Code s. 83.3(7)(c)(ii) — "when a person is taken before a provincial court judge under subsection (6) ... the judge may adjourn the matter for a hearing under subsection (8) but, if the person is not released under subparagraph (i), the adjournment may not exceed forty-eight hours."

12. The twenty-one-day period was authorized by Regulation 9.2 of the Public Order Regulations, 1970, enacted on October 16, 1970, under the authority of the War Measures Act; the seven-day modification was enacted by the Public Order Temporary Measures Act, 1970, passed November 2, 1970 (by a 152–1 margin).
13. Criminal Code s. 83.32.
14. Criminal Code s. 83.3(8) — "Recognizance with Conditions."
15. Criminal Code ss. 810.01, 810.1, and 810.2.
16. Martin L. Friedland, "Police Powers in Bill C-36," in Daniels, Macklem, and Roach, *The Security of Freedom*, 278.
17. Criminal Code s. 83.28.
18. Criminal Code ss. 83.28 and 83.29.
19. A. Alan Borovoy, "Does the Anti-Terror Bill Go Too Far?" *Globe and Mail*, November 20, 2001.
20. Criminal Code ss. 185(1.1) and 186(1.1).
21. CSIS Act ss. 2(c) and 12.
22. SIRC's duties are established and defined in the Canadian Security Intelligence Service Act, RSC 1985, c. C-23, s. 38.
23. Criminal Code s. 186.1.
24. Friedland, in Daniels, Macklem, and Roach, *The Security of Freedom*.
25. Canada Evidence Act ss. 38.03, 38.031, and 38.04.
26. Canada Evidence Act s. 38.131.
27. Canada Evidence Act s. 38.131(9).
28. Canada Evidence Act s. 38.15.
29. Canadian courts have held that the right to a "fair and public hearing" guaranteed in s. 11(d) of the Canadian Charter of Rights and Freedoms (Part I of the *Constitution Act*, 1982, being Schedule B in the Canada Act 1982 [U.K.], 1982, c. 11 [hereinafter Charter]) includes this obligation to acquit where excluded evidence would be vital to a fair trial. See, for example, *R. v. Seaboyer* [1991] 2 SCR 577, at par. 39, where J. McLachlin stated that "the denial of the right to call and challenge evidence is tantamount to the denial of

the right to rely on a defence to which the law says one is entitled."

30. Chief Justice Lutfy, in *Ottawa Citizen Group Inc. v. Canada (Attorney General)* 2004 FC 1052, par. 35.
31. Patrick Dare, "*Citizen* Reporter to Finally Get Her Day in Court: RCMP Raided Home, Office of Journalist," *Ottawa Citizen*, December 10, 2005.
32. *Ibid.*
33. Commission of Inquiry into the Actions of Canadian Officials in Relation to Maher Arar, *Report of Professor Stephen J. Toope, Fact Finder*, October 14, 2005.
34. Graham Fraser, "RCMP Raid Sparks Outrage," *Toronto Star*, January 22, 2004.
35. Security of Information Act, RSC 1985, c. O-5, s. 14(2).
36. Security of Information Act s. 4(1).
37. See affidavit sworn by RCMP Corporal Quirion on January 20, 2004, in order to obtain search warrants and orders sealing the warrants, Ontario Court of Justice, File No. 2003CID-4470.
38. Security of Information Act s. 4(3).
39. Foreign Missions and International Organizations Act SC 2002, c. 12.
40. Foreign Missions and International Organizations Act s. 10.1(2).
41. Ministry of Public Safety and Emergency Preparedness, *Government Response to the Twelfth Report of the Standing Committee on Foreign Affairs and International Trade (Security at Intergovernmental Conferences)*, February 2002.
42. E.N. Hughes, *Commission for Public Complaints Against the RCMP — Interim Report Re: APEC*, 441.
43. *Government Response to the Twelfth Report of the Standing Committee on Foreign Affairs and International Trade*, February 2002, 7.
44. *Ibid.*, 7.
45. McLellan, testimony before the House of Commons Standing Committee on Justice and Human Rights, October 18, 2001.

46. Anti-American protesters: "Hate Literature Charges Against 3 to Be Dropped," *Globe and Mail*, July 4, 1975; French Canadian nationalists: *R. v. Buzzanga and Durocher (1979)*, 101 DLR (3d) 488 (Ontario. CA); anti-apartheid activists: "Customs Pledges Procedure Review After Film Seizure," *Toronto Star*, December 26, 1986; pro-Zionist book: "Libraries Won't Ban Uris Book," *Globe and Mail*, October 11, 1984; the Jewish community leader: "Bronfman Is Target of Complaint," *Globe and Mail*, May 6, 1989.

47. Canadian Jewish Congress, brief to the House of Commons Standing Committee on Justice and Human Rights on Bill C-36, the Anti-Terrorism Act, November 6, 2001.

48. *Ibid.*

49. See Robert Wistrich, "Islamic Judeophobia — An Existential Threat," in *Nativ*, Vol. 15, Nos. 4–6 (87–88), September and November 2002, 49–53 (Part I), and 79–85 (Part II). See also Dr. Reuven Erlich, *Anti-Semitism in the Contemporary Middle East*, information bulletin prepared for the Intelligence and Terrorism Information Center at the Center for Special Studies, Israel, April 2004. Available at *www.intelligence.org.il/eng/sib/4_04/as_hp.htm#toc.*

50. As, for example, in Daniel Pipes, "The Danger Within: Militant Islam in America," *Commentary*, November 2001.

51. *Ibid.*

52. Daniel Pipes, "The Rot in Our [Canadian] Universities," *National Post*, January 30, 2003.

53. See, for example, Robert Fulford, "Elmasry's Fantasy Outrage," *National Post*, July 8, 2005.

54. Editorial, *National Post*, November 22, 2001.

55. An Act to Amend the Criminal Code (Organized Crime and Law Enforcement) and to Make Consequential Amendments to Other Acts, SC 2001, c. 32 ("Police Lawbreaking Act").

56. Criminal Code s. 25.1(8)(c).

57. Criminal Code s. 25.1(9).

58. Criminal Code s. 25.1(11).

59. Criminal Code 25.1(9).
60. Alexandra Highcrest, "Why The Mounties Don't Always Get Their Man — or Woman," *Eye Weekly*, May 19, 1994.
61. Controlled Drugs and Substances Act, s. 55(2.1).
62. "Mounties Planted Him in Western Guard, Painter Tells Jury," *Toronto Star*, November 23, 1977; "Broke Law 100 Times — Informer," *Toronto Star*, November 24, 1997; Stanley Barrett, *Is God a Racist?* (Toronto: University of Toronto Press, 1987), 89.

Chapter 4: The Adequacy of the Safeguards

1. Anne McLellan, testimony before the House of Commons Standing Committee on Justice and Human Rights, November 20, 2001.
2. Grant Obst, testimony before the House of Commons Standing Committee on Justice and Human Rights, November 1, 2001.
3. *Ibid.*
4. Anne McLellan, testimony before the House of Commons Standing Committee on Justice and Human Rights, November 21, 2001.
5. *Ibid.*
6. See, for example, Thomas Gabor, "The Views of Canadian Scholars on the Impact of the Anti-Terrorism Act," research report, Department of Justice/Research and Statistics Division, March 31, 2004.
7. Bill C-36, s. 83.32.
8. McLellan, testimony before the House of Commons Standing Committee on Justice and Human Rights, November 21, 2001.
9. Vincent Westwick, testimony before the Special Senate Committee on Bill C-36, December 4, 2001.
10. Patrick J. Lesage, "Report on the Police Complaints System in Ontario," April 22, 2005, Section 3, 23–25.
11. Westwick, testimony before the Special Senate Committee

on Bill C-36, December 4, 2001.

12. *Ibid.*

13. *Ibid.*

14. Police Services Act, RSO, c. P15, *passim.*

15. Bill 103, An Act to Establish an Independent Police Review Director and Create a New Public Complaints Process by Amending the Police Services Act, 2nd Session, 38th Legislature, Ontario, 2006.

16. The Royal Commission on the Donald Marshall, Jr., Prosecution, *Report,* Province of Nova Scotia, December 1989.

17. Report of the Aboriginal Justice Inquiry of Manitoba, Aboriginal Justice Implementation Commission, November 1999, Vol. 3, "The Death of John Joseph Harper — The Investigation": "Both at the scene of the shooting and during the subsequent interrogation, much more attention was given to protecting Cross than was devoted to uncovering the facts of the case."

18. "Police Ostracize Fellow Officer Who Blew Whistle, Assault Trial Told," *Toronto Star,* May 30, 1987.

19. For a survey of these kinds of attitudes, see *CCLA Submission to the Commission on Systemic Racism in the Ontario Criminal Justice System,* November 2, 1993.

20. Reid Morden, "Domestic Security: Finding the Balance," in *The Canadian Response to September 11th: Taking Stock and Next Steps,* a symposium jointly sponsored by the Robarts Centre for Canadian Studies and the Centre for Public Law and Public Policy, York University.

21. Criminal Code s. 83.31.

22. McLellan, testimony before the House of Commons Standing Committee on Justice and Human Rights, November 21, 2001: "Proper review and oversight of the powers provided for in Bill C-36 help ensure that the measures in Bill C-36 are applied appropriately."

23. *Ibid.*

24. Pierre Trudeau is quoted in J.L.J. Edwards, *Ministerial*

Responsibility for National Security (Ottawa: Supply and Services, 1980), 94–95.

25. Commission for Public Complaints Against the RCMP, *Hughes Report,* 451.

26. See for an examination of this phenomenon Kent Roach, "Four Models of Police-Government Relationships," July 2004, background paper submitted to the Ipperwash Inquiry. Available at *www.ipperwashinquiry.ca.*

27. Greg Joyce, *Hamilton Spectator,* August 31, 1995.

28. Attorney General Harnick is quoted in Ontario Hansard, April 1, 1996.

29. Premier Mike Harris is quoted in Ontario Hansard, May 29, 1996.

30. Testimony of Honourable Bill Graham, *Commission of Inquiry into the Actions of Canadian Officials in Relation to Maher Arar* (May 30, 2005), transcript, 4140–141.

31. Testimony of Honourable Bill Graham, 4142–143.

Chapter 5: Consequential Issues and Collateral Fallout

1. Bill C-18 s. 17(5).
2. *Canada (Secretary of State) v. Luitjens* (1989) 2 FC 125 at par. 44.
3. *Canada v. Baumgartner* (2001) FCT 970 at par. 8.
4. *Schneiderman v. U.S.* (320 US 118).
5. *Jaballah (Re)* TD 2003 FCT 640.
6. Jeremy Finkle, "Conscience in the Court," *Saturday Night* (Summer 2002).
7. *Ibid.*
8. Jeff Sallot, *Globe and Mail,* September 15, 2005.
9. Immigration and Refugee Protection Act, SC 2001, c. 27, s. 34(1)(b).
10. Immigration and Refugee Protection Act s. 34(1)(f).
11. *Ibid.*
12. Bill C-18, An Act Respecting Canadian Citizenship, 2nd Session, 37th Parliament, 2002 s. 21(1).

13. Bill C-16, An Act Respecting Canadian Citizenship, 2nd Session, 37th Parliament,1999–2000, ss. 21(1) and 22(1), as passed by the House of Commons but never enacted.

14. Bill C-18 s. 18(5).

15. Bill C-18 s. 28(e).

16. As reported in Hansard, 2nd Session, 37th Parliament, No. 059, February 13, 2003.

17. *Ibid.*

18. Ben Shneiderman's testimony before the Hearing of the U.S. Subcommittee on Government Efficiency, Financial Management and Intergovernmental Relations, November 16, 2001. See *www.aei.org/publications/pubID.17867.filter.all/pub_detail.asp.*

19. Tom Campbell's remarks are cited by, among other sources, James K. Glassman, *Washington Times*, November 4, 2001.

20. Ed Crane's remarks are cited by, among other sources, Doug Bedell and Paula Felps, *Dallas Morning News*, October 4, 2001.

21. Simon Davies et al., "Identity Cards: Frequently Asked Questions," Privacy International, August 24, 1996. See *www.privacy.org/pi/activities/idcard/idcard_faq.html.*

22. *Ibid.*

23. For a more recent assessment of the identity card issue, see "The Identity Project: An Assessment of the U.K. Identity Cards Bill and Its Implications — Interim Report" (London: London School of Economics and Political Science, March 2005).

24. Davies et al., "Identity Cards: Frequently Asked Questions."

25. Standing Committee on Citizenship and Immigration, 6th Report, *A National Identity Card for Canada?*

26. *Ibid.*

27. *Ibid.*

28. Donna Leinwand, *USA Today*, February 7, 2001.

29. Standing Committee on Citizenship and Immigration.

30. *Ibid.*

31. *Ibid.*

32. Stephen T. Kent and Lynette I. Millett, eds., "Policy Considerations," in *IDs — Not That Easy: Questions About Nationwide Identity Systems, National Research Council* (Washington, DC: National Academy Press, 2002).
33. Davies et al., "Identity Cards: Frequently Asked Questions."
34. *Ibid.*
35. Pentagon briefing paper, "Working Group Report on Detainee Interrogations in the Global War on Terrorism: Assessment of Legal, Historical, Policy and Operational Considerations," March 2003.
36. *Ibid.*
37. *Ibid.*
38. U.N. Convention Against Torture and Other Cruel, Inhuman or Degrading Treatment or Punishment, General Assembly Resolution 39/46, December 10, 1984, Part I, Article 2 (2).
39. Universal Declaration of Human Rights, General Assembly Resolution 217 A (III), Article 5; International Covenant on Civil and Political Rights, General Assembly Resolution 2200A (XXI), December 16, 1966, Part III, Article 7: "No one shall be subjected to torture or to cruel, inhuman or degrading treatment or punishment."
40. Kenneth Roth, "Bush Administration Lawyers Greenlight Torture Memo — Suggests Intent to Commit War Crimes," Human Rights Watch media release, June 7, 2004.
41. "The Harm the U.S. Does in Rationalizing Torture," editorial, *Globe and Mail,* June 12, 2004.
42. U.N. Convention Against Torture and Other Cruel, Inhuman or Degrading Treatment or Punishment, General Assembly Resolution 39/46, December 10, 1984, Part I, Article 1.
43. Christopher Hutsul, "The Temptation to Use Torture: How Far Would U.S. Go to Make Mohammed Talk?" *Toronto Star,* March 9, 2003.
44. See the following excerpt from the website of Human Rights Watch (*www.hrw.org*): "While the forcible administration of

so-called 'truth serums' — drugs such as sodium pentothal, sodium amytal, and scopolamine — does not involve the infliction of severe pain, its use to secure information from a person would nonetheless be prohibited under international law. Human Rights Watch believes that at a minimum it would violate the person's right to be free from 'inhuman or degrading' treatment. We note that Article 2 of the Inter-American Convention to Prevent and Punish Torture expressly defines torture as including 'the use of methods upon a person intended to obliterate the personality of the victim or to diminish his physical or mental capacities, even if they do not cause physical pain or mental anguish.'"

45. Hutsul, "The Temptation to Use Torture."
46. Alan Dershowitz, *Globe and Mail*, March 5, 2003; William Schulz, *Globe and Mail*, March 6, 2003; "Resisting the Lure of Expedient Torture," editorial, *Globe and Mail*, March 10, 2003.
47. Schulz, *Globe and Mail*.
48. *Ibid*.
49. Eric Schmitt, *New York Times*, June 16, 2002.
50. "The Legal Prohibition Against Torture." See *www.hrw.org/press/2001/11/TortureQandA.htm /press/2001/11/TortureQandA.htm*.
51. Alan Dershowitz, *Why Terrorism Works* (New York: R.R. Donnelley & Sons, 2002).
52. Schulz, *Globe and Mail*.
53. "Resisting the Lure of Expedient Torture," *Globe and Mail*.
54. Schulz, *Globe and Mail*.
55. Dershowitz, *Why Terrorism Works*.
56. *Ibid*.
57. Commission of Inquiry into the Actions of Canadian Officials in Relation to Maher Arar, *Report of Professor Stephen J. Toope, Fact Finder*, October 14, 2005.
58. Jeff Sallott, *Globe and Mail*, November 19, 2003.
59. Larry Neumeister, Associated Press, December 18, 2003.
60. *Ibid*. See also "Report of the Chair of the Working Group

on Arbitrary Detention: Situation of Detainees at
Guantánamo Bay" (February 15, 2006); *passim*, "U.S.
Committing Torture at Guantánamo, U.N. Says," *Globe
and Mail*, February 16, 2006.

61. The notion of creating a special extra-legal status for "enemy
combatants" was actually created by Franklin D. Roosevelt's
Proclamation Number 2651 and upheld by the U.S.
Supreme Court in 1942 (*Ex parte Quirin*, 317 US 1, 31, 37
[1942]). But the power thereby given to U.S. presidents to
declare enemy combatants was not used until the aftermath
of 9/11. See Larry Neumeister, *Associated Press*, December
18, 2003. See also Mark Isikoff and Mark Hosenball, "The
Enemy Within: How the Pentagon Considered Extending
Its Controversial Enemy Combatant Label in a Bid to Prove
Links Between Iraq and Al-Qaeda," *Newsweek*, April 21,
2004. In November 2005, the U.S. Senate voted to strip
captured "enemy combatants" at Guantánamo Bay, Cuba, of
the right to challenge their detentions in United States
courts. See Eric Schmitt, *New York Times*, November 11,
2005. See also memorandum from George W. Bush,
"Human Treatment of Al-Qaeda and Taliban Detainees,"
February 2, 2002.

62. In July 2006, the U.S. Supreme Court dealt a setback to the
encroachments on "due process" of President George W.
Bush's administration. In holding that the Geneva
Conventions apply to al-Qaeda prisoners taken in
Afghanistan, the court rejected the breadth of the discretion
the president had claimed in matters of national security.
While this case might well reduce the presidential proclivities I have criticized, it remains important to examine the
lengths to which those in authority in that country have
been prepared to go. It is also important to acknowledge the
viability of certain safeguards that American democracy continues to observe even in these troubled times. See *Hamden
v. Rumsfeld* (2006) USSC (No. 05-184).

63. James Risen and Eric Lichtblau, "Bush Lets U.S. Spy on

Callers Without Courts," *New York Times*, December 16, 2005.

64. "Even a War President Is Not Above the Law," *Globe and Mail*, December 31, 2005. In fact, the Federal Intelligence Security Act only rejected four of the over 19,000 government requests for wiretaps from 1979 through 2005. See testimony of Harold Hongju Koh, dean of Yale Law School, before the U.S. Senate Judiciary Committee Regarding Wartime Executive Power and the National Security Agency's Surveillance Authority, February 28, 2006.

65. Federal Intelligence Security Act, USC tit. 50 § 1805.

66. Stewart Powell, "Secret Court Modified Wiretap Requests," *Seattle Post-Intelligencer*, December 24, 2005.

67. Verified by Ron Grey, leader of the Christian Heritage Party, via email, March 10, 2006.

68. "With a concerted effort by each citizen, displaying love in action, Canada will become once more a God fearing and child loving Nation," Christian Heritage Party, "Position Statement on the Issue of Abortion" (*www3.telus.net/public/clabots/abortion.html*). "The Bible teaches that God gives life as a gift. Human life has inherent worth and must be respected and protected through all of its stages, beginning at conception," Evangelical Fellowship of Canada, "Social Issues: Abortion" (*www.evangelicalfellowship.ca/social/issue_viewer.asp?Issue_Su mmary_ID=11*).

69. Roman Danylak, "Choose Life: Reflections on the 30th Anniversary of Humanae Vitae," *Catholic Insight* (July-August 1998).

70. Wayne Kondro, "MLA's Support for Gays Brings Slur from Tory," *Calgary Herald*, July 5, 1986. According to the report, New Democrat MLA and Anglican priest William Roberts claimed that Stockwell Day said this to him. The press contended that Day said he didn't remember "using those exact words," but he reportedly did not deny making the statement.

71. Verified by Ron Grey, leader of the Christian Heritage Party, via email, March 10, 2006.

72. Canadian Council of Churches letter presented to the Right Honourable Pierre Elliott Trudeau, prime minister, on December 14, 1982.

73. William Coffin Papers, "It's a Sin to Build a Nuclear Weapon," *The Arms Race and Us* (from a conference at Riverside Church), November 15–16, 1981.

74. "Memorandum of Argument of the Proposed Intervener the Interfaith Coalition on Marriage and Family," In the Matter of a Reference by the Governor in Counsel Concerning the Proposal for an Act Respecting Certain Aspects of Legal Capacity for Marriage for Civil Purposes, as Set Out in Order in Council PC 2003-1055, July 16, 2003.

75. *Zylberberg v. Sudbury Board of Education* (1988), 65 OR (2d) 641; and *Canadian Civil Liberties Assn. v. Ontario (Minister of Education) (1990)*, 71 OR (2d) 341 (CA), "Elgin County."

76. School Act, RSA 2000, c. S-3, ss. 50(1).

77. See *www.2learn.ca*.

78. School Act, RSA 2000, c. S-3, ss. 50(1) and (2).

79. See note 75 above.

80. *James Chamberlain et al. v. the Board of Trustees of School District #36 (Surrey) (B.C.)*, 2002 SCC 86.

81. *Ibid.*

82. Demitry Papasotirou, "In Allah We Trust: Islam and Religious Fanatics Among Us," *Obiter Dicta*, March 12, 2001.

83. *Ibid.*

84. York University, "Presidential Regulation Number 2 — The Conduct of Students at York University."

85. Letter from Peter Hogg to A. Alan Borovoy, June 27, 2001.

86. Adrian Humphries, *National Post*, May 1, 2001.

87. Ron Csillag, "Jews Join Other Faiths at School Funding Rally," *Canadian Jewish News*, November 24, 2005.

88. See for an account of this process, C.B. Sissons, *Church and State in Canadian Education: An Historical Study* (Toronto:

Ryerson Press, 1959).

89. R.M. Williams, *Strangers Next Door: Ethnic Relations in American Communities* (Englewood Cliffs, NJ: Prentice Hall, 1964).

90. Access to Abortion Services Act, RSBC 1996, c. 1, s. 1 (definition of *protest*). Under this legislation it is possible that, by regulation, the government could draw the line more closely to any or all of the clinics. But that would be entirely within the government's discretion.

91. See, for example, *Elizabeth Bagshaw Society v. Breton,* 1997 Carswell BC 2472, par. 21, wherein the defendant was arrested for "maintaining a prayer vigil" inside a prohibited zone.

92. *Hellquist v. Owens,* 2006 SKCA 41. In 2006 the Saskatchewan Court of Appeal reversed the Board of Inquiry. But its decision was based entirely on whether the impugned article fell within the scope of the statutory prohibition. There was no "free speech" invalidation of the prohibitions themselves.

93. *Ibid.*

94. *Brockie v. Ontario Human Rights Commission* [2002] OJ No. 2375 (Div. Ct.).

95. *Ibid.*

96. *Congrégation des Témoins de Jéhovah de St-Jérôme-Lafontaine c. Lafontaine (Municipalité),* 2004 SCC 48.

Index

199